MW01006444

6/25

Seattle

amazon.com

# MOE NORMAN

# AMAZING STORIES

# MOE NORMAN

The Canadian Golfing Legend
With the Perfect Swing

BIOGRAPHY/SPORT
by Stan Sauerwein

PUBLISHED BY ALTITUDE PUBLISHING CANADA LTD.
1500 Railway Avenue, Canmore, Alberta  T1W 1P6
www.altitudepublishing.com
1-800-957-6888

Extreme care has been taken to ensure that all information presented in
this book is accurate and up to date. Neither the author nor the
publisher can be held responsible for any errors.

|                    |                   |
|-------------------:|-------------------|
| Publisher          | Stephen Hutchings |
| Associate Publisher| Kara Turner       |
| Series Editor      | Jill Foran        |
| Editor             | Dianne Smyth      |

We acknowledge the financial support of the Government
of Canada through the Book Publishing Industry Development
Program (BPIDP) for our publishing activities.

**Altitude GreenTree Program**

Altitude Publishing will plant twice as many trees as were used
in the manufacturing of this product.

**National Library of Canada Cataloguing in Publication Data**

Sauerwein, Stan, 1956-
Moe Norman / Stan Sauerwein

(Amazing stories)
Includes bibliographical references.
ISBN 1-55153-953-5

Cataloguing in publication data is available on request from the publisher.

An application for the trademark for Amazing Stories™
has been made and the registered trademark is pending.

Printed and bound in Canada by Friesens
2 4 6 8 9 7 5 3

Cover: Moe Norman, photographed in 1984, playing the game he loves.
(Photograph courtesy of the Canadian Golf Hall of Fame)

Some hear "you can't" and give up.
Moe Norman listened to a different voice.

# Contents

# Prologue

*The shoulder of the sled run at sombre-looking Kitchener Collegiate Institute was a scrambling swarm of freckle-faced youngsters that morning. Soaked to the skin but happy, scores of them had taken to the hill above Glasgow Road to slide. They zipped down the middle and then half-crawled on their knees back to the top of the steep slippery surface, chattering about their spills. It was the kind of winter day the kids, who lived just a few blocks away, dreamed about. Though it was cold, the hill was being dusted by powdery snow. That made for one sure thing. Speed.*

*The hill tapered into a flat tabletop run of 60 feet or more before it dropped sharply towards a two-lane road at the bottom. No one ever made it that far, so no one worried.*

*Marie watched her twin five-year-old brother, Murray, stuff his feet into the curved front of the toboggan. Two friends squatted down behind him. With the loop of rope at the front of their wooden chariot gripped tightly in woollen mittens, the boys nudged themselves off the lip of the hill towards their steep ice-covered plunge. The toboggan moved easily, gathering speed as it dropped. In that moment, all Marie could see was a blur of colour and a trailing spume of snow. The toboggan rocketed downwards but instead of digging in at the bottom as usual, it skimmed across the flat landing zone like a rock skipping over water.*

*Within seconds the toboggan had reached the drop-off where it gathered a new boost of momentum and vanished towards the road.*

*Marie watched in breathless panic from the top of the hill. The toboggan had slid across the street and into a driveway, coming to a stop behind a car. The driver was backing up, unaware the wooden missile had landed behind him. Horrified, Marie stared as the automobile reversed over the toboggan and then suddenly stopped. After hysterical seconds of stillness — thinking her brother killed — she could see tiny figures crawl out from beneath the car and run for home.*

*Though her redheaded brother was apparently uninjured, Marie and the rest of the Irwin family would eventually come to suspect the crash had somehow changed little Murray forever.*

*In the least, he certainly grew up to be different.*

# Chapter 1
# Life on the Other Side of the Tracks

They were called the "hard times." In the economically depressed 1930s, Kitchener was a city of grime and soot, slumped like a dirty blotch of black in the midst of some of Ontario's finest verdant farmland. Kitchener had been an industrial hub of the County of Waterloo since the middle of the 1800s when it was still called Berlin. Just an hour-and-a-half drive from Toronto, it was a culturally unique city. Industrious German immigrants with Mennonite heritage had marked it with their enterprise for more than 100 years. It boasted furniture factories, a distillery, several small breweries, and insurance companies. It was the kind of place where people worked hard and happily. But the presence of rubber companies such as BF Goodrich, Dominion Rubber, and Uniroyal gave Kitchener an infamous reputation. It was also a grimy place to live.

The factories in Kitchener belched black smoke that hung in a haze over the city and set down a blanket of soot over everything. The air always smelled of rubber in Kitchener during the years leading to and through the Depression. Though the people who lived there were grateful for the jobs the tire plants provided, no one ever got used to the stink.

Twins, Marie and Murray Norman, were born in the Kitchener pall on July 10, 1929, to a hardworking Catholic couple. Their parents, Mary and Irwin Norman, lived in a modest two-storey, red brick home at 57 Gruhn Street, almost within the shadow of the Uniroyal plant. The twins arrived just 10 months after brother Ron and a year before sister Doreen. In just over three years, the tiny Norman home, with its minuscule front yard and steeply pitched roof, had been transformed into a raucous nursery. It was a house filled with children's laughter, bolstered by two more siblings (Shirley and Rich) during the next 13 years.

The Norman household was an example of why the working class neighbourhood of Westward, where it was located, had been meanly nicknamed "Incubator Avenue." Homes were huddled close together, built for function more than beauty. Dominated by working class Catholic families, Westward streets were filled with giggles. Some families had as many as 10 or 12 children. Their fathers and mothers struggled to keep them fed and clothed and, like the other parents, the Normans managed most of the time.

Though not too far away in distance, Westward was completely different from Westmount, where plant managers and the pillars of Kitchener's business community lived. There were definitely two social strata sharing ground in the community of Kitchener in those days. To most of the children growing up on Incubator Avenue, Westmount was a different world.

When Marie arrived home after the accident, breathless and tearful, she found her brother cradled in her mother's arms. His face was swollen and red, but otherwise Murray appeared to be no worse for wear. The driver, gravely concerned for the young tyke, was trying, with the coaxing support of two police officers, to convince her mother and father to send Murray to the hospital. But visits to a doctor (before the Canadian government launched Medicare in 1966) were an expensive proposition. It was especially so for the Normans, who had to scrimp just to pay their $72 mortgage every month. Besides, Murray seemed to be okay, even though one of the car's rear tires had grazed the right side of his face as it passed over him.

In the years that followed, the Normans were said to have regretted their cost-conscious decision. As Murray grew up, he seemed to develop a frenetic kind of personality. Always hyperactive, he took to the worrisome habit of speaking very quickly and repeating himself. On rare occasions, it was claimed, he suffered mild spells that could only be described as convulsions.

Though an active nature never stopped Murray from doing whatever his otherwise healthy playmates were doing, his siblings knew their brother, with his fiery hair, was different. He preferred to be alone, existing with them but somehow apart, in a world of his own making. Murray was a loner, shy and introverted except when it came to athletics or thinking games. He had natural athletic talent that shone when physical co-ordination was required. If play turned to activities that called for memory or quick calculation, he also excelled. His aim was always deadly and his will to win unstoppable. The King Edward School playground across the street from where the Normans lived was the perfect environment for rambunctious Murray. When spring arrived so did baseball and little left-handed Murray was a star batter. With what seemed like effortless control and gifted hand-to-eye co-ordination, he was a mini Babe Ruth.

To his childhood friends, however, Murray came in a curious package. He had perpetually tousled hair, a carefree grin to match his dancing blue eyes, and big ears that grew out from his skull with a pronounced flare. He was a shy playmate with a melodious way of speaking that branded him as different. His words danced up and down the scale when he spoke and usually spilled from his mouth as quickly as he ran. Many had difficulty understanding him, even though he often repeated what he said with annoying regularity. He participated joyfully in any sport. Murray was one of those tough competitors who somehow managed to turn off distractions and perform with fluid natural ability as if nothing else in the universe existed at that moment.

Unfortunately, that superhuman focus wasn't so readily apparent scholastically. At St. John's Roman Catholic Elementary School, Murray also had trouble with social dynamics. He was shy and retiring in the classroom, excelling at the precise requirements of arithmetic, but little else. He demonstrated an astounding memory for numbers, and was able to see patterns and sequences easily. But when faced with giving an example of a gerund or having to explain a scientific principle, he would struggle. Murray found every subject other than math difficult to comprehend and seemed to lose interest. His academic failures in the classroom whittled away at his self-esteem. Apparently, as a result of this, he felt inferior to the other pupils and would refuse to offer answers for fear of ridicule.

In the schoolyard he became the victim of cruel taunts for the way he dressed and the hurried way he spoke. To the rest of the world Murray appeared mentally slow and his classmates reinforced that image. Over time, he began to think of himself as Dumb Moe. "Moe's a schmo. Moe's a schmo," he'd say to himself, and his classmates would join in with their chorus of ridicule.

Occasionally, Murray would react to the hurtful barrage, especially when he took part in a physical challenge. But not often. Instead, he retreated from situations and individuals that made him uncomfortable. He developed a deep shyness — fuelled by an inferiority complex and fed by his fear of ridicule — and his world shrunk. It became a place where only the known was welcome. New experiences could too easily turn into embarrassment, so he avoided them whenever possible. He wanted to live in situations that were always the same, situations where he had an element of control. His small circle of neighbourhood playmates became the only world where he felt safe.

Coming from a household with a modest income,

*Life on the Other Side of the Tracks*

Murray never had the taste of luxury. The meagre weekly allowance his friends received was rarely matched by the 10 cents or so Irwin or Mary might dole out on weekends. The result was a young boy who felt the need to acquire his pocket money himself. Murray learned to keep an eye open for opportunities. Earning change as a 12-year-old was not easy in the early 1940s, but Murray knew that the best place to look for it was where rich people were found. In Kitchener, that place was the golf course, a 10-minute bicycle ride from Murray's home.

The Westmount Golf and Country Club designed by Stanley Thompson, the same man who created the world-famous Banff Springs Golf Club, was the private preserve of Kitchener's moneyed class. Wealthy businessmen and plant managers used Westmount for sport and socializing. Compared to the streets of Westward, it was posh. Male players wore ties when they golfed the fairways carved from the surrounding maple and oak forest. When they weren't enjoying a genteel round, the decidedly British membership could often be found retired behind the club's stone gate, eating meals that the palates of blue-collar families like the Normans never tasted. The Tudor-style clubhouse was one of Kitchener's most prized locations for parties and celebrations. Being a member at Westmount meant you had achieved success in Kitchener. And that attracted Murray.

Before the advent of motorized power carts to scoot players from tee to green, the golfers at Westmount turned to the eager band of youngsters who gathered at the caddy pen near the driveway and pro shop to heft their heavy bags of clubs. Murray, though an under-weight and odd-looking boy, found a ready supply of change at Westmount whenever he showed up. A caddy for a nine-hole round cost golfers 30 cents. If they played 18 holes it was just less than double that, 50 cents. Usually the boys were tipped a nickel or a dime as well, and the very rich or happy golfing customer might even make that a quarter.

Murray showed up at Westmount whenever he could after school and on weekends. In the summer it became his second home, every day and all day. He was an eager caddie who was observant and attentive. But not always silent. He watched his golfers with the intent of a serious student. And despite Normie Hines, the Westmount golf pro, repeatedly cautioning Murray, he would often make whispered remarks about his golfer's skill loudly enough to be heard. Murray was not an assertive type, but when it came to something he could understand, he was confident and even outspoken.

Math was one such topic and golf, as it turned out, was another. Murray got good at spotting the most generous golfers. He had a simple technique to avoid having to caddy for the less well-off players or the ones who didn't tip. He simply hid in the bushes behind the wooden caddy pen and watched automobiles that arrived at the clubhouse. When he saw a golfer remove a good bag from the car trunk, he'd jump into action, ready to earn his tip.

His strategy didn't always work. Hines was savvy to the 'pick 'em' ploy. On one occasion, when a wealthy member who was notoriously miserly with tips arrived, Murray stayed hidden in the bushes. Hines insisted the boy appear to carry the member's clubs. That round was a test of wills.

Westmount, with its heaving landscape, demanded a lot of effort from the caddies who shouldered a heavy golf bag for 18 holes. If a caddy did well, found his golfer's lost balls, was quiet and yet attentive, he deserved a tip. Murray thought the tip was justified and practically obligatory, but this wealthy golfer didn't. After the round, when the member gave the skinny boy the standard two quarters for his services, Murray reacted in a style that was only characteristic when it came to golf. He tossed the change back at the golfer, reportedly telling the man in no uncertain terms that he appeared to need it more. Then he began hurling the man's clubs into a tree. To the golfer's anguish, several of the clubs lodged in the upper branches. On hearing of

Murray's conduct, a furious Hines banned the boy from the course for a month.

Even so, the fast-talking redhead became a favourite among the Westmount players. He knew the course and understood the game. He seemed to be supercharged, rushing down the course, and was always ready with exactly the club his golfer would need for his next shot. When asked, Murray could easily clarify the rules of the game. He could read the greens with certainty and was rarely wrong in his recommended club choice on a difficult lie. To a young man used to experiencing the opposite reaction from his schoolmates, the respect Murray got from players at Westmount was a meaningful boost to his self-esteem. Naturally, he loved it there.

Not long after he began to caddy, Murray starting skipping school on Caddie's Day (Thursdays) so he too could golf. Like many of the other caddies from humble households, Murray couldn't afford his own set of clubs. To help out the boys on Caddie's Day, some members would make their clubs available. However, Murray had a problem. He was left-handed and none of the *southpaw* members at Westmount were kind enough to lend their expensive and hard-to-find clubs to a hacking youngster. In desperation for his chance to play the game, Murray taught himself right-handed play with a swing that was opposite to his nature. Amazingly, in spite of that, he still played well.

Hines, who was a mentor to his squadron of caddies, took note of Murray's unquenchable enthusiasm for the game. He decided to let Murray and some of the other caddies buy their first clubs from his Pro Shop on a generous payment plan. The five-iron Murray chose cost $1.50 to own, and was paid for over time at a dime for every round that Murray caddied. He used it constantly and eventually the regular playing members at Westmount who noticed took pity by gifting Murray with their battered hand-me-down clubs as well. During his early years at Westmount, Murray also gained a caddy nickname — Moe the Shmo. Murray didn't mind, since that is what he called himself. Gradually, the name became the more affectionate, shortened version, "Moe." It seemed to fit the pleasant but strange boy perfectly.

# Chapter 2
# The Swing is Born

Moe enjoyed golfing more than anything else he'd ever done. To him golf wasn't a pastime as it was viewed by the golf course membership. It was a sport and it was a sport that demanded skill. To gain any kind of dominance in the game meant practice and Moe wanted to play Westmount more than once a week so he could get better. Unfortunately, Moe's father, Irwin, was not a member and Moe had no hope of ever seeing his father become one. But Moe and a few of his caddy friends were so eager to play they didn't let the restrictive access at Westmount stymie them. They soon discovered there was an alternative.

## The Swing is Born

In 1935, as the Depression gripped Kitchener, the City Fathers decided to make use of the plentiful man-power that was sitting idle at the Union Halls. The city council's make-work solution was to build a public golf course with out-of-work men under the direction of city engineer, Stanley Shupe. For less than Moe was earning only five years later to caddy nine holes, the men worked all day. They slowly transformed what had been a low-lying sewage overflow area at the edge of town into a golf course using nothing more than picks, shovels, and rakes. When Moe was 12 years old, the course was an immature version of what it would eventually become, but it was a fine golf course just the same. Rockway Golf Course came to represent one of Ontario's best public golf venues. It had a modest but charming wood-frame clubhouse dressed in pale stucco, set on the course's highest point overlooking the 18th green. The best feature, as far as Moe was concerned, was the fact that Rockway was just a two-penny ride on the King Street tramline to the eastern edge of Kitchener.

The course was unique in the world of Ontario golf because it was built for the working class to enjoy. It was a friendly place where junior players could learn from their elders and it had a special added feature in its head pro, Lloyd Tucker. Tucker seemed to understand that the future of the game rested in the hands and hearts of the scraggly bunch of youngsters who were flocking to his greens. He welcomed them, nurtured their interest, and offered them guidance.

With a wallet full of saved tips, his motley collection of old clubs, and the prospect of more golf than he could handle, Moe turned his back on Westmount and headed to the outskirts of town. For 10 cents, Moe found he could play 18 holes. The taste of freedom on the fairway wasn't satisfying with that short a round though. He often stretched the banquet to 36 holes, then stuffed himself on 54 and even gorged on 72 holes in a single day. He would race around the course with eager urgency, completely focused on his game.

In his early teen years, golf had become an almost unhealthy obsession for him. All the money he had went back into the game. He would forget to eat or refuse meals if that meant time away from the fairway. While his friends were bulking up in size, he remained skinny and short. But at his age and skill level, size was not a factor in golf. He could play as well as his bigger friends and do it with style. The game fed his appetite for competition. He could do it his way and even win, without a coach barking orders or team members shouting recriminations. At home this intense preoccupation began to create friction between Moe and his father.

Moe saw no reason why teeing up balls on Irwin's

tidy front lawn was a problem. After all, he rarely took divots that were too deep, and the balls usually tracked over the chain link fence of King Edward Elementary School across the street anyway. It was worse when he and his friends ventured to the schoolyard for the range practice though. The grass in the field was usually unmowed and high, so Moe and his friends would first spend some time cutting it to fairway height with their irons until they had etched a little square, and then hit from there. In two years, Murray's drives smashed 11 windows in houses along Gruhn Street and his father reportedly took out compensation for the glass replacement on Moe's backside.

The physical punishment was only occasional though, and did not deter him. Murray continued to swing, sending balls zinging along the street's pavement, up driveways, and through windows. Golf was something he could do *well* and he enjoyed that feeling. He certainly wasn't getting that satisfaction in school. While arithmetic continued to come easily to him, the rest of the curriculum he was forced to endure in his junior high school years was torture. And he still didn't fit in.

While other boys his age were discovering girls, Moe spent time by himself reading comic books. He also loved to play cards because, as with math, he had an incredible memory for them and could consistently win. He found a similar joy with bowling and billiards because they required the same kind of eye-to-hand co-ordination he was honing with golf. Besides those things, nothing else mattered, especially not schooling. He knew too well that his parents could never afford to send him to university anyway. Murray tried to explain why golf meant so much to him when his parents berated him about his passion. At least with golf he had a chance in life, he'd tell them. With golf, maybe he could get good enough to compete. Maybe he could win money. Maybe he could be rich and famous...more rich and more famous than the rest of the family combined.

That idea coming as it was from a young teen, was ludicrous to Irwin and Mary. Golf was not a career for heaven sake. Golf was a just a game, and worse yet it was a rich man's game. Golf was for bosses or bankers, not for a working stiff who put in an honest day's labour in the rubber plant, or at a shipping dock like his father was doing. Out of frustration for Moe's singular focus on golf over schoolwork, Irwin banned golf clubs from the house, at one point even reportedly burying the clubs in the backyard. It was an easily overcome hurdle for Murray. He simply dug them back up and found a way to store his clubs out of his father's reach under the front porch.

## The Swing is Born

The battle of wills continued as Moe got older. By the time Moe reached high school, the running argument with his parents had become a sliver embedded in their relationship, and it was getting deeper all the time. Moe was skipping his Grade 9 classes at St. Jerome's High School so often that the school district's truancy officer demanded the Normans *force* Moe to go to school. When they did as they were ordered however, it revealed a stubborn streak in Moe. All his life he'd been turning away from conflict, be it on the schoolyard or in the classroom, but this was one time he didn't. Insisting that Moe attend classes he hated was precisely the one thing his parents should not have done. Rather than comply, Moe refused to return to school — ever again.

In spite of a weak Grade 9 education to call upon, Moe quickly managed to find a menial job at one of the city's rubber plants. With it, Murray had no other restrictions in the way of his golfing dream. He worked as much as the piece-work position would allow, and spent the rest of his time at Rockway or Westmount. Though he continued to live at home, that existence was for convenience only. Moe reportedly often arrived at the house after the rest of the family had retired and would leave again in the morning without a word. It was the way Moe handled conflict. In Moe's eyes, if his parents ridiculed his passion for golf, they were ridiculing him.

And, just as he'd always dealt with the bullies, he turned away from Irwin and Mary.

Murray spent $10 to become a junior member at Rockway and immediately became a fixture there. Because he wasn't attending school, he was noticed. That, and his odd way of dressing as though he didn't care in the least what he wore — wrinkled, dirty, or mis-matched — gave him a level of notoriety. The Rockway members called him "The Kid," and for the most part, enjoyed his antics.

When the weather made playing golf impossible, Moe found an equally enticing diversion in the locker room. Playing cards for money. Moe quickly built a rep-utation with a deck, playing almost instinctively. He had a photographic memory, which made games like Gin Rummy a lesson in wizardry for his opposing players. Many of the older members of the club learned to hide their wallets when Moe was about on a rainy day.

When his piece-work job petered out, Moe found more regular work at the Kaufman Rubber Company factory. He rotated his time between making boots, swinging clubs at Rockway, and setting pins at The Strand Bowling Alley on King Street. When he turned 13, The Strand became his winter season hideaway. The thin young man was as dextrous as a monkey in the narrow working parts of the lanes. As a five-pin pinsetter earning two cents a line, the job at The Strand demanded speed and concentration.

Most pinsetters managed two lanes at a time. The task required them to monitor the bowlers in each of their lanes. They'd leap down between the lanes from a short wooden platform at the end of each frame, scoop up the pins, and reset them before the next bowler sent another ball flying. Moe was an expert. He was able to speed-shift among four lanes, basically doubling his pay. He was *fast*. Bowlers often tipped him for his speed, and every nickel he earned he counted like a miser. He had to make sure he could afford his golfing passion.

Juggling jobs became a normal way of life for him. But golf always took precedence. Moe's dedication to the sport was more like religion. Everything else came second. Kaufman's was a good example. When Moe began to play in club tournaments the irregular shifts he got at the factory cut into his time on the links. Eventually, he called in sick once too often and was fired, but he let that disturbance in his schedule pass without concern. All he needed to do, he reasoned, was fill the time differently.

Now in his late teens, with some factory experience to point out in the employment interview, he managed to secure another assembly line job at the Dominion Rubber Company. This time though, it was on the night shift. It was a perfect fit for Moe. During the day he could play and at night he stitched boots. A good fit for a shy boy. For eight hours he could work on the line, building up the strength in his left hand with the repetitive stitching motions, talking to no one, thinking only of golf.

The introduction of a steady pay envelope didn't change his outward appearance, however. Moe continued to be thrifty, almost to a fault. He continued to arrive at Rockway in tired, sometimes soiled, clothing that rarely matched in colour or style. He continued to scour the ditches for bottles and the fairway rough for golf balls so he didn't have to spend his hard-earned money to buy them. And he continued to line up in the Westmount caddy pen to heft golf bags. To anyone who observed the red-haired ball hawk, Moe was a sad example of a poverty-stricken youngster. Members often took pity on him and Moe rarely tried to dissuade that emotion. He allowed them to buy him his favourite drink, Coca Cola, or candy. And why not? After all, every penny he spent was a penny that could not be applied to golfing.

Even with his constant practice, however, Moe was not getting any better at the art of the game. At 16 he could best be described as a hacker, never able to consistently break the 100-stroke barrier in a game. He became frustrated that he was only occasionally able to sharpen his game to the 80s, and was never able to beat Gerry Kesselring, one of the other boys at Rockway. By 1945, Kesselring had won the junior title at Rockway twice, scoring rounds of 80 or less.

Moe began to concentrate on what he decided was the most important part of his game. Rounds on the course became secondary to putting in time at Rockway's driving range. He dissected his swing, and researched the mechanics by observation and by discussion with other golfers. Moe's biggest problem was his hook. He decided that it was caused by allowing the club face to move off-line and concluded the remedy was simple. All he had to do was stop the club from wiggling. He began to practice by gripping it for dear life.

He told his friends he was "trying to squeeze the blood out of it." His resulting grip was more like holding a baseball bat, and the unconventional technique immediately began to show results. Within a year he'd shaved 20 and then 30 strokes off his game. In Moe's obsession with golf, he started to focus on nothing more than his swing and the secrets of achieving consistent purity. Practice on the range translated directly to results on the course. Moe came to the conclusion that practice was what he needed, what anyone hoping to become a champion golfer needed. Moe became a monk acolyte at the altar of the swing.

# Chapter 3
# Practice
# Until It Hurts

D aily, Moe attacked the Rockway driving range with his canvas bowling-pin bag filled with 600 balls. The weather didn't matter. In the rain of springtime, in the blazing blast-furnace heat and humidity of summer, in the chilly winds of autumn, Moe made it to the range every day. His routine was always the same. He became almost mechanical, driving his balls with an inhuman rhythm. Hit. Place...Hit. Place. The cadence was like the ticking of a clock, rarely more than three or four seconds between swings. Moe's quirky nature had Rockway members shaking their heads. They concluded the driven young man was a few clubs short of a bag.

Practice Until It Hurts

Yet, the chuckles and whispers didn't affect Moe's dedication to his practice regimen, at least not outwardly. On the range he was in his *zone*, searching for perfection and struggling to force muscle memory of that moment so it could be repeated. Hit. Place...Hit. Place.

Anyone who watched couldn't help but come away astonished. He was doing everything wrong. Moe had his legs spread wide apart. He stood away from the ball far enough to force himself to do an exaggerated reach. He set up his back swing at least 18 inches behind the ball instead of gently beginning right behind the tee. And he did everything fast. No wiggles in advance to cue himself. It was as though he was in a striking race of some kind. Hit. Place. Hit. Place. Weighing just 140 pounds, Moe obviously called on all the energy his thin body could generate for every swing — and he did it without a break — for hours at a time. The long cords of muscles in his thin forearms became clearly defined ropes beneath his freckled skin. The white visor he constantly wore turned a stained yellow from years of sweat that dropped from his reddened face in a constant trickle during practice. Moe's technique became mechanical. He would take a quick glance down the range, find a target, and set himself. Three-quarter back swing. Swing. One ball barely had a chance to land before he was ready again. Hit. Place. Target. Swing...Hit.

35

Place. Target. Swing. It went on consistently for a long enough time to send any observer away muttering. He was phenomenal.

When the canvas bag was finally empty, Moe would trudge down the range and refill his bag of smiles. If he still had energy, he would do it all again...1200 balls. And sometimes again...1800 balls. When he was exhausted, he'd finally make his way into the Rockway clubhouse, happy.

He was a student of his body, observing it with almost cold indifference to pain. After a session, his regimen included plunging his arms and hands into hot water. By noting which of his muscles hurt the most, he was able to determine which were being overworked. He would mentally analyze his swing, the muscles in his back, his legs. He even tried to gauge which eye seemed more tired than the other. Everything was judged and considered in a quest to correct the problem the next day. In a visionary fashion, years before visualization became an accepted technique to improve athletic performance, Moe was creating mental pictures for himself. He was watching the movie in his head and noting everything. The flight of the ball. The split-second co-ordination required for his unorthodox swing. In a way, Moe was designing his body to be a striking machine, sculpting the muscles for optimum

power and control. He was training his mind to antici-
pate and then expecting his body to perform the perfect
swing.

To help it along, he invented drills. To keep his club
face on line for as long as possible, Moe would place a
coin 40 inches in front of the ball and another 20 inches
behind it. He'd then practice his swing so the club
passed over the coins. The sessions could last for hours.
His swing was so precise the soleplate on the front and
back of the club became marked by the coins. His goal
was to make the effort mechanical and ingrained.

Moe also focused attention on his *tools*. He reasoned that, like a hammer, his club head should be
heavy. Carpenters used the mass in a hammer's head to
multiply the force of their swing to drive nails easily and
straight. In his assessment, the same reasoning could be
applied to golf. A heavier club head should help to
reduce waver on the down stroke. Moe experimented.
He layered lead tape to the backs of his clubs, assessing
the differences it made to control and distance. The
weight forced his larger muscles to work and increased
the strength in his forearms.

He also tinkered with the design of his irons, grind-
ing the leading edges down so they were square and
bending the heads to reduce their loft. It made his drives
low, but it also added one more element to perfect

control. And he began using super-stiff shafts. He peeled the standard leather grips off his clubs and wound tape around the shaft to thicken them where he choked the club, extending the grip length downwards 30 per cent more than the standard length. Then he replaced the leather with rubber grips. He designed his clubs with his muscles in mind and they became the perfect extension of his swing.

He didn't wear a glove in his practice sessions. The almost manic effort often left his palms bloody and raw. After his *heat test* in the clubhouse, he would soothe his hands in cold towels, then patch himself up with bandages, and the next day attack his session with the same vengeance. Over time, his palms became thickly calloused, so much so he had to trim down the toughened skin with razor blades so he could grip the club properly.

Through it all, he was driven to achieve without the support of his family, or even his closest friends. Some told him that golf was a "sissy" game. A few members at Rockway, who noted how much time he spent at the course, suggested he ought to be working instead. None of them realized that to Moe, this was *work*, that golf was the career he'd chosen for himself. On the range the only critic was his inner voice. Fitting with his nature, he was happiest there, with that inner companion. Moe had a stubborn almost fanatical dream to become the best ball striker alive. And the rest of the world could go to hell.

The level of resolution and will about golf and his swing was completely uncharacteristic of Moe, a young man whose self-assurance was often measured in how quickly he turned from a stranger or avoided a new experience. The swing he developed felt right for him and that was all that mattered.

On the course, Moe and his friends, Gerry Kesselring, Gus Maue, and Tony Matlock, could charge through 18 holes in two hours. The other boys could outdistance their thin opponent on drives, but Moe was always more accurate. He hit straight. How far the ball went became a matter of his selection of a target on the fairway.

At the age of 19, Moe won the first tournament of his career. He was partnered with Kesselring to win the 1948 Ontario Junior Better-Ball Tournament at the Summit Golf Club. Moe felt good about what he called "the move" that season. He didn't have to think it through anymore. He was not fumbling, as his competitors did, to correct minor changes that crept into the fluid swing rhythm. Moe's machine was tooled, oiled, and running perfectly. Every time he swung, he hit the ball the same clean way. His swing never varied. It was pure. Sweet. Moe realized that the secret to success was simply hard work. He'd perfected the simplest move to be found in golf and was ready to show all his past detractors how wrong they'd been.

Although Moe Norman was a veritable encyclopedia when it came to the rules of golf — and he respected the game for the science of technique and mental control that it is — he never fell into the common mold expected by the golf establishment or by the fans. Moe didn't subscribe to the convention that said golfers had to look or act a certain way. He had his swing and a library of shots he could call up in his mind to fit any situation he found himself in on the fairway. That was all that should have mattered, in his opinion.

It seemed that life itself sometimes conspired to make Moe appear different and strange to everyone. He wanted desperately to be recognized for his skill but no one seemed able to look past the caricature that he unthinkingly portrayed. His arrival at the Canadian Amateur in Hamilton, the same year as his Better-Ball win with Kesselring, was a case in point.

Travelling to the tournament, the Rockway players' auto broke down as they entered the City of Hamilton. They were late. Missing their tee times would spell disaster. An angel in the form of a garage mechanic saved them by volunteering to drive the foursome to the Hamilton Golf and Country Club in a dump truck. They arrived in a cloud of blue smoke, two boys standing in the back of the truck with their golf clubs, just in time for Moe's tee off.

Moe ran to the tee box as they called his name. In a flurry of arms and legs, his face blossoming into even more red than his normal pink tones, Moe unceremoniously dumped his bag, extracted his driver and skipped forward in his black high-tops. Using his frantic driving style, he pounded his ball and then carried on as if that was exactly how all his rounds began. It was one of the few tournaments he could afford to enter that year. But, as part of the legend he was building, that arrival would remain one of his most memorable.

Moe took that winter to make money pinsetting at The Strand and the following season was ready to enter every tournament he could. Three days before his twentieth birthday, Moe took part in the first St. Thomas Golf and Country Club Invitational Tournament ever held. The St. Thomas organizers had invited the best golfers from private clubs in Ontario to participate. The field included Jack Nash and Nick Weslock, both Ontario amateur champs. When Moe hitchhiked to the St. Thomas club, he didn't have an invitation but was hopeful of a post-entry spot, and got one. He was equal to the rest of the field, he thought, but the entry was about where similarities ended. The other players in the tournament dressed to fit their parts. They were well-heeled country club golfers who had gathered to show their refined skills.

Moe Norman arrived on foot, lugging his tattered canvas golf bag which was scarred with tape and grime. He would be carrying it that day while other competitors strolled the fairways with a caddy. He played in his running shoes. If anyone needed a visual image of an "amateur," Moe was it. Except for his clubs. In that department he showed his elite frame of mind. By this time he'd acquired a set of Bobby Jones clubs from a Westmount member. He carried them with pride and swung them with consummate skill.

Though he'd never played the course before, Moe took it apart that day scoring a 67. His round was two strokes better than the expected winner, his friend Weslock, and four strokes better than three-time Ontario amateur champ, Nash. It was his first individual win and should have been cause for celebration by the young man. Others would have basked in the tide of congratulations. Not Moe. Upon signing his card and passing it over to the scorer, Moe headed home. Winning was enough to him and besides, hitchhiking with a golf bag after dark would be impossible.

Naturally, the organizers were appalled by the lack of social grace demonstrated by Moe's absence at the award ceremony. Weslock, who'd golfed with Moe many times, stood in for his friend explaining to the gathering in the clubhouse that The Kid was talented but extremely shy.

A few weeks later, Moe wowed the gallery again by winning the Twin-Cities Tournament in Kitchener and Waterloo, which was held at the Westmount club. For Moe it was an even greater achievement than the round at St. Thomas because he won in front of a hometown crowd. His achievement was covered in the newspaper and it gave him a small taste of celebrity among the Westmount golfers. Moe was beginning to ride on a wave of self-esteem and he took that energy with him to the Kawartha Invitational in Peterborough not long after. There, he beat another triple Ontario amateur champ, Phil Farley, in a 54-hole test.

That season, Norman, Kesselring, and Matlock were winning wonders. They captured tournament titles so often that the players at Rockway dubbed them "The Three Musketeers" — Matlock, who had grown up on a farm beside the course; Kesselring, who was considered one of Canada's top players; and Norman. It seemed that whenever a title was to be decided, the final outcome always came down to one of them. But playing together so often resulted in a competitive disadvantage for Moe. The other young men knew Moe had a soft under-belly when the game was on the line. It was his self-esteem. With a few well played holes that indicated luck or skill might not be on his side, Moe's confidence could be dulled. It made him beatable more often than a difficult course did.

During the 1950 Ontario Amateur Tournament held at the Toronto Golf Club, Matlock proved it. His round was pure poetry on the greens and Moe's winning resolve vanished. It wouldn't be the last time that happened.

Moe appeared to question his abilities when faced with a player he respected. It was almost as though he gave up. He appeared to deliberately miss putts, evidently trying to hasten an end to his agony. When he played Kesselring the outcome was practically a foregone conclusion. To Moe, Kesselring seemed to represent a missing side of himself. Although Kesselring was also a quiet young man, he always managed to call upon a reserve of self-confidence when confronted with a new social situation. He easily gave speeches in front of strangers, and could warmly chat with organizers and fans. He seemed to play with an expectation of victory and he won consistently. Kesselring claimed nine junior or amateur titles from 1945 to 1953 and Moe idolized his golfing buddy for that skill. When they played together casually, they flew around the course in a happy state of bliss. Moe always tried to beat him but never managed it. Though he could match Kessy shot for shot, on the greens Moe never measured up. For every hour Moe spent at the driving range perfecting his drive, Kesselring spent equal amounts of time on the practice green. His short game exemplified supremacy compared to Moe's. "Can't beat Kesselring, can't beat Kesselring," Moe would tell Weslock and others. "Too good, too good."

Still, trying to beat his idol gave Moe a personal goal. It was as though he had established a measurement of improvement for himself and he never stopped trying. Strangely, when opportunities to do so actually presented themselves in a match, the reluctant winner always showed his head. Moe seemingly missed putts intentionally or placed his drives so that recovery without extra strokes was impossible. Perhaps he feared the results of a win against such a top-ranked player. More media attention, the need to speak to strangers and answer questions. It all made Moe very uncomfortable. All he wanted to do was put the ball in the hole and go home. He was never shy on the course, but get him off it and he reverted to his reserved and private persona. He knew it was something he should work on. But he also knew he couldn't change.

# Chapter 4
# Facing the Challenge

Once he'd reached his early twenties, Moe seemed to have found a comfortable groove in his golfing and in his lifestyle. He competed in numerous tournaments during the season, winning many, but had not yet achieved an important career milestone such as winning the Ontario Amateur title.

Even so, the press loved him. He represented a colourful side of golf and his unorthodox manner of play was something different for sports reporters to cover. Instead of a loose almost fluid stance, Moe's was rigid. Instead of a long thoughtful assessment of the fairway before striking the ball, Moe was almost cavalier in the tee box. While his well-dressed competitors took a full back swing, Moe lifted his club head only three-quarters of the way back and then uncoiled with such speed his arms were a blur. He sent his ball sailing unerringly straight every time, unless he purposely wanted to play a fade. He always finished like he was reaching for the sky and then charged after it, rarely waiting for the ball to land. Other golfers might sneer or scowl, portraying a fierce competitive concentration in the tee box, as if the movements they were about to make were sacred. Not Moe. He turned into a performer when he entered the tee box with a club in his hand. He might chat with a fan or make a comment about the weather. "Great day to golf, great day." It was always obvious he was cheerful at the prospect of doing what he enjoyed.

On the greens, he was even more of an entertainer. He walked confidently to his ball and tapped. If it was within a foot-length he might backhand it into the cup as if it didn't matter. "Just a game, just a game," he'd say and move to the next tee. Should the gallery be slow, he might have teed off before they arrived.

Hilles Pickens, the editor of *Canadian Sport Monthly*, wrote that Moe's "seeming lack of concern while reducing a tough layout to a 'soft touch' induces a distinct inclination to burn one's own clubs and take up croquet." The fans were awed by his drives. They were always pure and straight and rocketed exactly to where he was aiming. Often the fans would laugh with glee. Moe, however, only heard ridicule. The press called him "Golf clown Moe Norman" and he resented it, but rather than alter his image or his style, Moe embellished on the image.

The fairway and tee box was a stage and Moe, while on it, "turned on." It was as if he didn't realize that his antics actually fed the uncomplimentary impression he was creating. He'd joke with fans and perform his tricks...bouncing a ball off his club and into his pocket or strolling the fairway tapping the ball like it was attached there by an invisible rubber band. His record was nearly 200 yards walking and tapping. He even held up play with dextrous demonstrations and once, at a tournament in Belleville, Ontario, took a bet with a spectator on the number of times he would tap without missing. To Moe, it was all about adding a little colour to the game, helping his audience have as much fun as he was having.

As a teenager he'd perfected another stunt. It made him famous as a performer. The only problem was the gallery failed to see that what he was doing proved his swing purity. Like an audience asking for a card trick over and over in the hope of seeing how it is done, the gallery was amazed by the stunt. But they forgot the years of hard work Moe had invested to enable him to perform it. Moe Norman had a selection of oversized tees that varied in height from four to eight inches. To the urging of his audience he would set up with one of them and rifle his shot down the middle of the fairway to the "ahhs" and "oohs" of the crowd. Or he might simply drop a ball on the tee, step on it for good measure, and then drive it perfectly.

While it may all have added spice to a round, Moe's comedy performances riled many of his competitors. He was detracting from the professionalism of the sport, demeaning all of them by making golf seem too easy. Even some of the devotees who followed the leaders around a course reacted negatively. They complained angrily about his pace or were offended when he didn't concentrate more on the greens.

To Moe it was just their tough luck. He usually ignored hecklers, as he had the bullies in the schoolyard. However, when for some reason a loud fan said something negative about his style that particularly annoyed him, Moe would explode. He'd rain a torrent of vulgarities on the fan and visibly fume. It spoiled his game because he deeply resented criticism. To Moe, it was unfair and impolite behaviour. He looked to the galleries of other great players and saw fans respectful. He saw how they hushed when those players swung a club, how they clapped at even the poorest shots, and he wanted the same reverence.

Among tournament organizers, Moe's behaviour was considered unacceptable. As he won more and bigger tournaments and performed his skills, he caused golf-governing bodies, usually headed by the blueblood of golfing, to reject rather than accept him for what he was. They simply didn't appreciate his public course attitude, the way he dressed, the way he milked the crowds for laughter. No one in authority could argue that Moe was lacking in golf talent, but it was the rest of the package that didn't fit their mold. Moe was a character. And they saw him thumbing his nose at all the social trappings of their precious game.

Here was a man they couldn't reason with. Ever. And he had terrible teeth — badly in need of dentistry — their deterioration hastened by a steady diet of Coke. He wore rumpled sometimes soiled clothing. He made no bones about a course's condition or a tournament's officiating. And when officials had the nerve to complain, he only got worse. In short, he was more trouble than he was worth. They simply didn't understand him.

All that mattered to Moe Norman was golf. All he wanted was to hit the ball purer than anyone ever had. When, in the clubhouse, members veered their conversation from golf to anything else, Moe blanked out. He would shrug and wander away. He just didn't understand politics or follow the latest movie star gossip. Moe was lucky if he knew the prime minister's name.

Any situation that pulled him from his secure world of golf made him nervous. He didn't want to appear foolish in social situations such as press conferences or receptions. His anxiety when standing in front of an audience anywhere but the golf course made him physically ill, so he took the easiest solution. He avoided it all. Even trophy presentations.

That created even more friction between Moe and tournament officials. Organizers wanted their champions on display after a tournament. They wanted to congratulate and be congratulated. It was the way of things — but it wasn't Moe's way — and it may have been the biggest hurdle in his quest to become Canada's best golfer.

"If I had won the Canadian Open, I wouldn't have been at the presentation," Moe once told a biographer. "I was too shy then. I knew I would have had a fight with an official. He would have grabbed hold of me. I'd have given him a karate chop right in the shoulder. Whap! I know I would."

When Moe began selling his prizes, the golfing royalty were further incensed. At the time of Norman's rise in the rankings, the term "amateur" was considered sacred. Amateur golfers were just that. Amateur. They did not profit in any way from their wins. However, for Moe, being an amateur was more a state-of-mind than anything else. He considered himself the best ball striker alive and took to the fairways to hit golf balls with the attitude of a skilled professional. Golf was his career, even if he wasn't carrying a piece of paper that proclaimed it so.

Moe was one of the busiest amateur golfers in Canada in his early twenties. He was averaging 30 tournaments a season and winning 75 per cent of the time. Unfortunately, as an amateur he had to fund his competition. He had to pay for his transportation and accommodation. He had to fork over his hard-earned pinsetting cash for entry fees. The silver plates and watches he received as prizes didn't help him do that. So, Moe took what to him was a logical and common-sense approach. He sold his prizes for cash.

The Royal Canadian Golf Association's (RCGA) rules that defined a player's status as an amateur forbade the selling of prizes. To the RCGA it was a simple way to stop professional golfers from competing with amateurs. It evened out the field. Moe thought the rule was impractical. Besides, he could see the rules being flouted by other so-called amateurs all the time. Many he played against either came from wealthy families who could fund the players' activities, or they were business professionals who could personally afford the cash outlay. In Moe's case, with parents who didn't support his dream in the first place and could not have supplied the cash he needed even if they did, Moe had to either earn his playing season income himself as a pinsetter during the winter, or find another way.

His solution was selling his prizes, often right after a tournament win and in full view of spectators. Fans who might want the set of luggage he'd won, or the golf bag, could get a fast transaction in the parking lot for cash. For a time, governing officials turned a blind eye, but Moe wasn't satisfied with doing deals after a game. Justifiably, he had so much confidence in his play that he began to negotiate the sale of his prizes even before a tournament took place. He was so sure of his performance, he even began to take orders if a second or third place prize was the merchandise his buyer had an eye on. It was all done without guilt. Moe needed the money to continue. Plain and simple. He had to live, he told himself. How many times could he sleep in bunkers at a course because he didn't have the money to pay for a motel room? How many times did he have to settle for a plate of spaghetti or a hot dog and Coke as his one meal of the day?

*Moe Norman*

The term "poverty" was no exaggeration for Moe. As a young man he had owned only two pairs of pants. One was for golf and the other for church. He hitchhiked everywhere, relying on golf-friendly motorists who would see him at the roadside with his bag of clubs and take pity.

The RCGA rules, while well-meaning, didn't take into consideration a struggling young golfer like Moe Norman. He won three times as many wristwatches as there are time zones in Canada (often wearing several of them at the same time), and enough television sets to put one in every room of the house at 57 Gruhn. Was he supposed to watch them all? The RCGA said yes.

Luckily, the officials at individual clubs who organized tournaments took a more lenient view. Moe drew crowds with his antics and his play. He was good for business. Often, after a local tournament, Moe could be encouraged to put on an exhibition at the driving range. His performance was magical and the crowds that gathered would occasionally respond with contributions of change to a hat that was quietly passed from hand to hand. Moe flaunted the rules, and his fans knew it, but the fans also knew the young man was fighting unfair financial odds. The same support came from Rockway members as well. When a big tournament was in the offing, the most generous among them would contribute to his travel expenses, providing the cash to Moe's mother as an indirect means of getting around the RCGA strictures.

Many of the stories about Moe's suffering have been called suspicious by friends who knew better. Some stories, they said, were spawned by jealous private-club players who wished to use such tales as a way of ridiculing Moe. Regardless of the extent those stories may or may not have exaggerated Moe's situation, clearly, Moe did not have it as good as other golfers. Sacrifice was the cost of participation for him. And he paid it gladly.

# Chapter 5
# The Stuff of Champions

On the course, Moe was a traditionalist about the rules of the game. Though he might object to the snobbish pretensions that decked the fringes of golf at the clubhouse, he never ignored the rules of the game. He was a consummate gentleman with other players and adhered to the code of conduct. Golf was his religion and he played it by the rules. Golf etiquette was his sacrament. He searched for ways to compliment the men he played with during a round. He cheered their successes and sympathized with them when they duffed, always finding something positive to reinforce. "Off line, but good distance, good distance," he might say when a ball was shanked into the rough. It's against the rules to offer or take advice during a tournament. Moe never had to ask for advice, but he often pushed the envelope on the other side of the scale when it looked like advice was needed.

By the time Moe Norman was 25, he was finding the sureness of his stride among the giants of amateur golf in Canada. His game was consistent and superb. He was winning an unbelievable number of tournaments (at one point he lost only three of 19 events). Moe was playing at an elite level that put him shoulder to shoulder with the professionals. He was the Number One amateur in Ontario.

The RCGA, despite the governors' derogatory opinion of Moe Norman, could not pass him over when it came time to select the members for the Canadian players in the 1954 America's Cup. The America's Cup was an international showcase of the very best amateur players in Canada, Mexico, and the United States. Moe had worked his way into the ranks of the elite. And his record earned him the right to demonstrate that he just might be the best among them.

That summer, for its second running (and the first for which Canada was playing host) the match was held at the London Hunt Club in London, Ontario. In the America's Cup, the six players on each team competed over a two-day period. On the first day, the players from each team played in foursomes with the two teammates from a country alternating shots. On the second, each teammate had the chance to show his individual skill in match-play.

The RCGA had invited Moe reluctantly. The red-head was unpredictable, and the RCGA governors were concerned about his habit of showmanship and his manners, which they thought unbecoming to the vaulted status given the participants. The America's Cup, for them, had a lot to do with national pride and bragging rights.

When the practice round arrived, their worst fears were given form. Moe was not anywhere in sight. Team captain, Jim Anglin, led a desperate search and Moe was found at the St. Mary's Golf Club north of London, playing in another tournament. He didn't think missing the practice round was important since he was familiar with the London course anyway, having played it numerous times. The small tournament he was participating in was offering a new suit to its winner — and Moe needed one. Commonsense choice. So he entered. The rationale was patented Moe Norman.

The RCGA officials back at the Hunt Club saw it differently. Once Moe was hauled off the St. Mary's course and driven back to London, he was sequestered with the officials in a private room and served up a tongue-lashing. His conduct was not acceptable. Didn't Moe understand? There was press from both continents at the America's Cup. It was an honour to have been selected for the Canadian team and they begged him to settle down. Play golf, they ordered. Then, to push home their disappointment in his untimely participation at St. Mary's, the officials yanked Moe out of the first day's action.

On the second day, Moe was paired with Carlos Belmont of Mexico and Bill Campbell, an American who that year had been a finalist for the British Amateur Championship. For the betting crowd, Campbell was the hands-down favourite to win. He was the secret weapon of the U.S. team and one of the world's best amateur golfers. Like punters at the Kentucky Derby, they compared the players. Campbell was tall and handsome. An ice man in match play, he was tough, confident, and impressive. Norman was a skinny short kid from a public course somewhere in Canada, with a reputation for caving in under pressure. Campbell was a press darling, trim and athletic. Norman was a shy loner with forearms that looked like he could pose for a Popeye cartoon.

Moe, however, was not concerned. Unlike the times he played alongside competitors he thought were better, in this match Moe was the definition of confidence. He knew that Campbell was aware of his record of wins and his reputation as a pure ball striker. He knew that the Huntington, West Virginia amateur would come out of the gate skittish and feeling tremendous pressure to win. The RCGA tried to hedge their bets. They asked Keith Kirkpatrick, the club captain from the private Highland Golf Club in London, to run interference for Moe. His job was to keep the gallery away and prevent distraction, and to bring Moe around if his play turned errant. Everyone watched the game with tense anticipation of another "Moe episode."

With 18 holes played, Moe was three strokes behind Campbell but had edged his way to one stroke off Campbell's score by 16 holes later. On Hole #34 Campbell's drive put his ball just 20 inches from the pin. It was a brilliant shot. But by then Moe was in his zone. With an eight-iron, he swung for the flag target. His shot dropped three feet past the pin then spun backwards right into the cup for a hole-in-one that evened the match. The men remained even on the next hole, and on the 18th green Campbell missed a putt that would have given him the match. It shook his otherwise cold demeanor. Campbell's drive on the first extra-hole trickled. For his second shot, trying to regain ground, he sent his ball diving into water. Moe, of course, hit as true as

*The Stuff of Champions*

ever and managed to hold it together on the green. Norman's victory not only astounded detractors, it left his RCGA critics gasping. The one player they worried about most had given Canada an upset win. Though the U.S. still beat Canada in the Cup by a single stroke, Moe's performance was undeniably the single most thrilling part of the entire match. The *Toronto Telegram* coverage that followed lauded Norman and so did Campbell himself. He said Moe was "potentially one of the greatest players of our time."

The following year, Moe was once again the top-ranked amateur in Ontario and the national sports press classed him as the second-best player in Canada, after Doug Bajus of Vancouver. Early that summer, he proved that the sports writers should have had that ranking the other way around.

In June, Moe played in the Brantford Invitational at the Brantford Golf and Country Club and rocked Canada's golfing establishment. Another Stanley Thompson designed course, the par-72 Brantford Golf and Country Club was one of the most revered championship links in the country. Moe tore the course apart in his first round of play, scoring an unimaginable 9-under par. His second round was not as dramatic. He carded a 71, but won the tournament with a glorious 10-under par.

Riding on a wave of incredible performance, Moe finally felt ready to take his place in the records of the Ontario Amateur Championship. His old nemesis, Gerry Kesselring had turned pro, leaving Moe without the dogging shadow that always darkened his play. So, that July at Westmount — when Moe made the finals — he was unbelievably ready. An estimated 1500 fans turned out for the final match between Moe Norman and Jerry Magee, which was a record for attendance at the Ontario Amateur.

Jerry, like Moe, liked to play his game fast. Magee fit Norman's style exactly. They had the gallery running to keep up. With just two holes left in the match, Moe was one stroke up on Magee. On the 17th hole Magee managed a long 30-foot putt to tie them up, and the two men left the last hole even, forcing extra play. Magee's putter was sizzling and he did it again, sinking a 21-foot putt shot to win. The game was a tough one, with luck playing a role on both sides, but Moe's failed attempt to win the Ontario Amateur, on a course he'd caddied so often, was more grist for his detractors. They criticized him for his speed, for his lack of concentration and care on the greens, and put his loss down to a character flaw. "He fools around too much," they said.

The comments hurt Moe deeply. It seemed no matter how well he played, he could not shake his image as a clown and a golfing dilettante. But, because he came in second at the Ontario Amateur, Moe was again named to the Willingdon Cup Team for his province. He would be allowed to play in the 1955 Canadian Amateur, which was to be held at the Calgary Golf and Country Club.

The 6400-yard Calgary Golf and Country Club had been scratched from the prairies 30 years before. It was lined plentifully with trees, providing a relatively short narrow course. The layout's length and tight fairway targets made it the kind of course well suited for Moe. Other players' accuracy was tested there. But, after firing a pair of 69s with his pure straight drives, Moe was getting bored.

The gallery could sense his frustration, and knowing his reputation for breaking the boredom of slow play with some fun, called on Moe to provide a little entertainment by using one of his oversized 8-inch tees. Moe hummed and hawed. He refused the crowd's coaxing, telling them he'd promised his friend Nick Weslock (the Ontario team captain) he wouldn't use the 8-inch tees during the Willingdon Cup.

The crowd showed its disappointment, which seemed to spark a little fire in Moe. His blue eyes twinkled and his mouth, a picket fence of misaligned teeth, gave the gallery a rascally grin. "How about a six-inch tee?" he asked. It was a comic invitation. The crowd erupted in applause and Moe happily extracted a somewhat smaller but still gigantic tee from his bag and hit his drive with his characteristically hurried style. Of course the ball went precisely where all of his other drives had gone before. Right down the middle.

Moe played his rounds like a machine and was finally pitted against Lyle Crawford, two years younger and half-a-head taller. The morning play was an up and down battle between the two players. The competition was running without a hitch. Moe had refrained from surprising officials with ball bouncing and monster tees. He was playing at the greens like he meant to win. At the break for lunch in the clubhouse, however, the RCGA officials noticed something was amiss. Crawford was pleasantly chatting with the press. Officials were congratulating each other on a job well done. It was just the way mid-match lunches should run. Then they realized Moe was nowhere to be seen. Fearing a replay of his St. Mary's side-trip in London, the officials began a search. No, Moe was not at the range tuning up his swing. No, Moe was not in the locker room having a relaxing game of Gin. Where the hell was he?

The search became frantic as time approached for tee-off on the afternoon's resumption of play. Finally, they saw his red head between the trees. Moe, happy to avoid the crush and conversation of the luncheon, had sneaked away to the banks of the Elbow River. He'd relaxed there with a case of Coke and was dangling his toes in the water.

That afternoon, Moe played with ease. "Just a walk in the park, walk in the park." He had a fat two-stroke lead after the 15th hole. Crawford managed to chip that down to a one-stroke by the final hole. On the 18th hole, Crawford birdied to Norman's par and tied up the game.

It had turned into another nail-biting extra-hole battle, and everyone wondered if Moe could reprise his America's Cup finish. But Crawford didn't collapse as Campbell had done. The men both scored pars on the first extra-hole. On the second, Moe had a two-stroke lead, but he hurried his putt, actually stroking while Crawford was marking his ball, and left his ball five feet short. He then missed his second.

On the third hole, Moe's second shot put him nearly six feet from the cup. He moved to the green as Crawford chipped his ball to within 20 inches of the pin. His opponent's ball had only stopped rolling when Moe, fast and sure, tapped. His ball rolled like it was on rails. Moe Norman had just become the Canadian Amateur Champion.

Tumult erupted around him. The Kitchener wonder was mobbed by ecstatic fans and had to be pulled from the crowd. Once he was away, he retreated to his secluded hideaway on the riverbank and didn't return to the clubhouse again. He couldn't face the outcome. Just as he'd so often feared, the win put him into circumstances that were intolerably alien to his shy side. Crawford ended up accepting the championship trophy on Moe's behalf, and only after much coaxing by RCGA officials did Moe agree to pose for photographs.

# Chapter 6
# Blowing the Masters

I n some families, achievements are marked by celebrations. They have special dinners or offer gifts as mementos of the glory. They take photographs and share happily in the moment of a family member's success. They show their pride. In the Norman household, however, it didn't turn out that way.

When Moe crossed the tarmac at the Kitchener Airport, he was looking for his parents among the crowd of well-wishers who had gathered, but none of his family were there waiting. In Moe's eyes, it was as if his parents didn't recognize the Calgary win had even happened, and that hurt him deeply. Shyly showing his happiness anyway, Moe joined the crowd of Rockway members who were waiting. They transported him in a raucous horn-honking cavalcade to the club. The boy who used to heft their clubs for 50 cents a round was a now their hero. Even the mayor turned out to congratulate Kitchener's native son at an impromptu party arranged in his honour at the clubhouse.

Moe didn't know it at the time, but his parents had made an effort to join the celebration at Rockway. In the clubhouse Moe was treated to a highly charged dose of fame. While he was more gracious and outgoing than normal, it was a situation far too public for Moe. He managed to say only a few thanks, shake only a few hands, before the pressure was too much for his retiring painfully shy side. While members made speeches extolling Moe's performance, he slipped away from the crowd to be alone. Mary and Irwin arrived at Rockway a few minutes after his quiet departure. Thus, they were denied the chance to show their pride in Moe's accomplishment. He never saw their joy. He remembered only his disappointment.

Moe spent his winter after the win as he always did, setting pins at The Strand. He needed the money. Perhaps he hadn't been offered a different job by any of his so-called supporters at Rockway. Perhaps he felt most comfortable doing what was familiar. Regardless,

January found him in the bowling alley.

As the Canadian Amateur Champion, Moe spent the cold weeks setting pins and nervously waiting for his invitation to the Augusta National Golf Club for the Masters Tournament — the world's most prestigious golf competition. He'd been dreaming about it all his life. He'd vowed to his mother and father that one day they would see how the "sissy game" would make him rich and famous. And that day was about to arrive. But the letter didn't come for weeks, and when the formal invitation finally arrived in the mail at Rockway, Moe was sick of winter and sick of waiting. The lag time between seasons did serve to help him fatten his savings but it was also, and more importantly, time away from the game. He always had to work hard in the spring to recoup. So, a few weeks after he excitedly opened the envelope containing his invitation, Moe left Kitchener and his family. He resolved to spend the winter golfing in a warmer climate with two Toronto amateurs, Irv Lightstone and Ken Jacobs. Jacobs had been given a car by his father and the trio used it to travel in the southern states.

Their home base for golf became Brunswick, Georgia, where they shared rooms for $30 a month. The pro at the Brunswick Country Club kindly allowed the young men to play at the course for free. Moe was in heaven banging out his daily quota of 600 balls under the Georgia sunshine. It was the second time that Moe had joined Irv on the southern golfing getaway. But, while Moe had some savings from his pinsetting, they were hardly enough to finance months of golf, and the source of his wealth was a great mystery to Irv and Ken.

His secret was a man named Conn Smythe. The owner of the Toronto Maple Leafs had watched Moe play in the Labatt Open at the Scarboro Golf and Country Club and had taken a shine to the unorthodox young man. Moe was a character and Smythe liked characters. In Moe's attire and playing style, Conn Smythe saw spirit — and guts. When Moe won the low amateur in the tournament, Smythe had apparently taken a personal interest in him. Not long after, the irascible hockey icon gifted Moe with $3000, which was enough for Moe to finance his 1955 winter golf in Florida. It was against all the RCGA rules. And he did it again in 1956. Without Smythe's continued support giving him an opportunity to play, Moe may never have managed to break through to an individual championship.

Shortly before the Masters event, Norman decided that he wanted to learn the Augusta course because he thought it would help him with his play visualizations. Irv Lightstone drove him to the manicured lawns of the clubhouse a week before the golf tournament was scheduled. Moe played 45 holes every day, and was often the first to tee off each morning.

The entire week of the Masters is filled with social functions for the players. Augusta National members represent some of America's wealthiest industrialists and leaders of finance. The swirl of receptions is the members' chance to mingle with the best professional golfers on earth, and that year they welcomed the opportunity with enthusiasm. Moe, of course, eschewed the receptions. Instead, he played his rounds and then hit his golf balls on the range every day until he was exhausted.

Accommodation was provided for the invited amateurs in what was called the Crow's Nest, a small furnished dormitory in the clubhouse attic. Though the Crow's Nest was equipped with six beds, none of the other amateurs invited to the 1956 Masters needed to accept Augusta's charity. Players such as the British Amateur Champ, Roger Wethered, spent the days in advance of the tournament in expensive Augusta hotels. Moe had the single bathroom in the dormitory and the eye-watering "masters green carpet" that covered the dormitory floors all to himself.

When the Thursday start finally arrived, Moe was honed — but far from ready. He'd not slept well in the days leading up to his historic debut because he was wracked with anxiety about the galleries; 30,000 people curled around the greens and tee boxes. The prospect of the tournament being televised was also giving Moe butterflies. It would be the second time the important event was broadcast on television and Moe knew that in only a few hours he would be participating in something historic for golf. A Masters tournament. The dream of his lifetime.

Because of his status as the Canadian Amateur Champ, Moe was paired with his U.S. counterpart, Harvie Ward, as was the Masters tradition. They were followed by Byron Nelson and Cary Middlecoff (who was the defending champion).

Moe was terrified as he waited in the tee box for his chance to drive. Even before the announcer had completed his introduction, Norman had whacked his ball towards the middle of the fairway and was on his way. While his drives were pure and sweet, he found himself again plagued by errors on the greens. After his round, Moe had logged three-putts six times but finished with a respectable score of 75. It didn't place him at the top of the amateur rankings that day, but as the fourth-best amateur, he still had a chance. The next day, however, it was as though Moe was mentally reliving his Thursday opener. Luckily for him, there was no cut in the Masters' field in 1956. His game got worse by three strokes the second day and he was a staggering 18 shots back of the leader, San Francisco's wunderkind, Ken Venturi.

Moe knew he needed to burn off nervous energy. So, as always, he headed for the driving range. It was probably the one time in his life when the driving range was not his friend. As he hit his balls with rhythmic cadence, the legendary Sam Snead took notice and watched. After a few minutes, Snead offered Moe a tip on how to correct what he thought was a technical error in the swing. Snead was one of Moe's heroes. He had won the Canadian Open in 1938, 1940, and 1941. He'd won the Masters twice in the previous four years. A tip from Slammin' Sammy had to be right, Moe reasoned. All this time he'd been hitting the ball wrong.

With his powerful focus, Moe hit ball after ball after ball trying to adapt his swing to Snead's pointers. Hours passed. Moe's hands turned into pads of blisters and yet he still hit balls. In four hours, Moe churned through 800 of them before finally deciding to quit and go to bed. The next morning it was plainly obvious just how much he had overdone his practice. His hands were throbbing, bloody, and swollen.

Moe tried to play through the pain for his third round but his condition was excruciating. He was barely able to summon the strength to grip the club, and the shooting pains racing up his arms when his palms clenched destroyed his concentration completely. As he played the first nine holes that day, his stroke was completely gone. He botched his short game. He cursed himself under his breath for being such an idiot, but it was too late. When Moe realized the voice in his head was ridiculing him — just like his critics had been doing all his life — he mentally surrendered.

After his putt on the ninth hole, he turned away from the course and headed towards the locker room. Irv Lightstone, who was following Moe alone through the round, tried to turn him back. He urged Moe to "Think!"…this was the Masters. You don't walk off the course in the Masters! But Moe had made up his mind. He couldn't grip a club. There was no way he could continue.

When Lightstone told Moe's opponent for the day, 1941 PGA champion Vic Ghezzi, what his friend had decided to do, the veteran was appalled. "This is the Masters," Ghezzi answered like an echo. "You play on one leg if you have to." Ghezzi was forced to join the twosome following them and Norman and Lightstone headed back to Canada.

It was a heartbreaking setback for anyone who knew and supported the shy golfer from Kingston. That year he had repeatedly shown the world just how good he was at the game. He had set nine course records (he shot 61 on four occasions) and won 17 out of the 26 tournaments (a 65 percent win ratio). Despite his achievements on the record books, the black mark of Moe's disgrace in Augusta would be the only thing anyone remembered.

Outwardly, Moe didn't let the Augusta experience change him. But, to his acquaintances, it was obvious that Moe felt a need to prove himself again by winning the Canadian amateur championship a second time.

The 1956 championship was being held at Edmundston Golf Club and it attracted a field of 64 players. They were some of the best amateur golfing talents in the United States. The field included 24 Americans and the winner of the Canadian Open, Doug Sanders. Moe had no difficulty reaching the finals, where he was paired for the third round with Ed Meister. The weather was foul for the entire tournament, but it was at its worst on the second day when rain relentlessly poured down on the Atlantic Canada course.

For the third day the greens were fast and slick. Through the round the two men played even golf. For Norman's championship fights, this seemed to be standard. It continued into the first of the extra holes. But on the second Moe made a 12-foot putt to win. He took the win philosophically, simply shrugging and walking off to the driving range. For him the real tests were yet to come.

Moe took the quarter-round easily. In the semifinal, he roared, carding a 64. It was a masterpiece of golfing skill, with nine pars and nine birdies highlighted by four putts over five feet. After 29 holes, Moe finished his opponent, John Miles of New York State, with a 13-under score. For once, Moe was relaxed with his win, and even consented to meet with the press. "That was probably the best round I ever shot in my life," he said happily.

In the final, Moe got to play his friend Jerry Magee again. They golfed like they were jet propelled, doing the first nine holes in just 58 minutes and the second half in 60 minutes. The faster Moe played, the better he played and he won his second title carding 31-under par for the week of play. This time Moe didn't disappear. It was one win he wanted to accept himself — though he delayed the award ceremony by loitering at the practice green in what appeared to be a purposeful slap at his critics in the RCGA.

When he accepted the Earl Gray Trophy, Moe didn't say a word in gratitude. It was obvious to most that he'd proven he was the best amateur in the country, maybe even the world. He had no one to thank for that but himself. He left the opportunity for speeches to another

Rockway player, Gary Cowan, who had won the Canadian Junior title.

# *Chapter 7*
# Turning Pro

**M**oe Norman's homecoming was bitter this time. He flew back to Toronto and then, by differing accounts, either drove himself home or hitchhiked to Kitchener. Sadly, no celebration was waiting for the two-time hero. Perhaps it was because of his disappearance during the first win's party. Perhaps it was because the members at Rockway thought Moe would rather not be embarrassed by a celebration in his honour. Regardless, the fact that nothing was organized to acknowledge his win dulled Moe's feelings for the people he thought were his friends.

Moe's Canadian Amateur Championship victory automatically qualified him to play in the U.S. Amateur

Championship. Canada's golfing establishment was eager to show up its American cousins again and Moe was playing better than he ever had. Strangely, Moe never took the challenge of supremacy to the American event. He forgot to file his entry by the deadline. Whether it was an accident or an oversight has never clearly been determined. Moe and the RCGA got along only with thinly disguised courtesy. The RCGA seemed reluctant to push Norman forward in public as their champion, and Moe would not dance to their tune regarding image and style of play. It was a situation where, in hindsight, a little humility by the golfer may have made his future career development smoother. But it wasn't to be.

After the embarrassment of not having an entry in the U.S. Amateur, governors at the RCGA may likely have been looking for payback. Unintentional, planned, or otherwise, it came in the form of the next America's Cup, slated for Mexico. Moe was excited about participating. Mexico was exotic for one thing, but the America's Cup was also his chance to truly reach for the brass ring and be recognized as the top amateur in the world. If he could win. However as the Cup date approached, it became obvious that the RCGA was investigating Moe's past, looking for proof that he had been breaching the rules that defined amateur status.

That meant accepting money for appearances or expenses. And that meant profiting from his prizes as an amateur.

A year earlier, the RCGA had warned Moe about performing his exhibitions. More often than not, Moe benefited from the kind donation of a few dollars towards his expenses. The RCGA knew it and so did the rest of the golfing fraternity. The warning stuck with Moe but evidently too late. Rumours of the RCGA investigation suddenly exploded into press reports. Before long, a newspaper was even claiming the rumour that the Canadian government was on the hunt to collect taxes from all the cash Moe had gained passing the hat at his trick-shot exhibitions.

The president of the RCGA, Jim Anglin, claimed to have attempted to contact Norman for an explanation about his income and that he was unable to get in touch with him. Four days before the America's Cup matches, the RCGA decided to pull the plug on Moe. In an official statement, Anglin suspended Moe from the team because of evidence that Moe's activities had "cast serious doubt" on his status as an amateur. On October 19, Anglin is quoted as having told the *Toronto Telegram*, "I have telephoned repeatedly to his home in Kitchener and wired him offering to go to Kitchener to see him any time. Moe has not replied in any way."

Moe's colourful personality was unusual
on the professional golf circuit

Was this statement a result of ample evidence that
Moe had been selling off his prizes, or was it a suspicion
that the amateur had received cash from Conn Smythe?
Neither was officially detailed by the RCGA, but the
mess didn't sit well with Canada's golf fans. To them, it
appeared that by being yanked from the Canadian team

Moe was being penalized unfairly, that the bluebloods were coming down on a golfer who didn't match their vision of a champion.

Moe denied the claim that the RCGA had tried to contact him, saying that the first inkling he had of his suspension was the newspaper report. In Moe's opinion, the RCGA took action simply because he was winning so many tournaments and his calibre of play outshone the other amateurs. For one thing, it gave the world the impression that Canada's pool of amateur talent was shallow, which didn't reflect well on the RCGA. For another, Moe believed the RCGA knew he would never kowtow or change his style to fit their expectations. Because they didn't want him as their poster boy, he believed the RCGA was quite willing to make an example of him regarding amateurs and their income.

It was not an issue that would get resolved easily, even with a public apology, should Moe have deigned to give it. Moe suddenly had his purpose in life stolen, his dreams had been squashed in a most impersonal way. The America's Cup action was a crushing disappointment. Furthermore, the RCGA had made it clear by their stance that Moe would no longer be welcome at amateur competitions. Moe knew he had only one alternative if he wanted to play golf. He had to turn pro. And that scared him. He didn't have the money to travel and there were no sponsors in sight. Moe didn't want to climb the rungs of the RCGA qualifications for professional status either. However, he was hearing rumours that unless he declared his intentions the RCGA was going to force the matter by officially declaring him ineligible as an amateur. Like it or not, he had to force himself out of his comfort zone.

It took some time for Moe to act. After Christmas, however, he made the announcement that he was turning pro. In a letter of notice to the RCGA in January 1957, Moe Norman admitted to finding the "means of paying my expenses in order to play competitive golf. " He said what he had done was "possibly" a mistake and that he wanted to surrender his amateur status to be classed as a pro. The rules to attain that professional classification were straightforward. Moe had to obtain a Class B1 assistant card and work for a recognized full-time pro with a Class A card for five years. Only then would his status be elevated to professional. Moe's problem was that no club pros were knocking at his door with job offers. He had a reputation as a disheveled player who didn't get along easily with strangers. Sure, he could play golf exceptionally, but his swing style was contrary to everything about technique being taught at golf courses around the world. None of the full-time pros wanted to work with Moe Norman and, to be honest, Moe didn't want to work with them either.

The whole dilemma left him in limbo. He was neither amateur nor professional. Embittered, Moe headed
to Georgia. While staying with friends in Brunswick,
instead of playing tournaments he kept his game sharp
with "bootleg" golf. In many ways, bootleg is the golfing
version of pool hall hustling by cue sharks. Popular in
the southern states at the time, many good players
would take on all-comers for money and play for a set
amount per hole. Moe's unorthodox style was ideal for
the hustle. Hotshot players would look at his unkempt
appearance, believe him when he'd describe his game as
average, and eagerly take the bait. Moe was so talented
with ball placement, he could drag out their impression
for a few holes by intentionally making poor shots
before attacking his stiff's purse. It was a shady kind
of life, but to Moe it was the only living he could make
from golf.

In spite of his retreat at the Masters the previous
year, the Canadian amateur champ was again invited to
participate in Augusta that April. Moe's conduct in 1956,
his physical condition aside, had left many of the
Master's organizers with a bad impression of amateurs.
It was suspected that many didn't want the amateur
invitation tradition continued. Coincidentally, the
organizers were being pressured to make room for more

PGA Tour pros in the limited field allowed at Augusta National. Within a few years the habit was discontinued. Even the apparently automatic CPGA invitation was withdrawn, and in 1957 the organizers added a new twist to the match. The cut.

Moe attacked the event as he did any other on the opening Thursday. His drives were flawless, but he fell apart at the greens. He carded an unimpressive 77 on his first round and his second the following day was only a little better with a 74. Moe was among the first golfers to be cut from the Masters.

After his lacklustre reappearance in Augusta, Norman returned to Ontario. He invested his time in practice at Rockway, taking in a few minor tournaments and offering exhibitions. At 28 years old, Moe still had to hitchhike. He neither owned a car nor had a driver's licence. In spite of that, he managed to earn a small income by providing golf lessons and selling equipment in the parking lots at driving ranges in various locations across southern Ontario. His new business enterprise was not welcomed by the established club pros. Moe was underselling them on golf clubs and he didn't have the overhead expenses they faced as businessmen. Even his mentor, Lloyd Tucker, wanted Moe taken to task on the matter, but it didn't stop the young vagabond golfing wonder.

He continued to play at Rockway and enjoyed rounds with his golfing buddies, including Gary Cowan. On July 16, Moe joined a threesome to play 18 holes that carried a 10-cent-per-hole side bet with Cowan. It was a day that golf historians would analyze and talk about in clubhouse lounges for years to come.

For Moe, the round was just another "walk in the park." He enjoyed the light-hearted chat on the fairway and found himself in the zone. After the first six holes he was one-under par and suddenly he could do no wrong. He eagled the seventh and followed that with two birdies. It meant he finished the front nine in an astounding 30 strokes.

For the back track, he started with a bogey but recouped on the 11th hole with a birdie. By the time the foursome approached the 18th hole, Moe was carding a 10-under. Playing 59 on a regulation course was a feat of legendary proportion. Moe placed his shot just six feet from the hole and gently tapped in his putt for the course record at the time (his golf card has been bronzed and remains on display at Rockway to this day).

With that staggering round a clear memory, Moe entered the Canadian Open being held at Westmount. He felt a solid confidence in his game, probably more than he'd ever had. He was two strokes behind the leader after 36 holes, but his performance declined in the final. He carded only two 72-stroke rounds which slid him to the rear of the pack and netted him a paltry $150 cheque. Still, Moe was happy. He could see he was able to play with the best and had the right stuff to win. All he needed now was money to tour.

A bursary tournament funded by British and American Motors was his chance. The tournament, organized under the auspices of the Canadian Professional Golfers' Association (CPGA), was created to provide the three top players with enough money to play in the U.S. PGA winter tour for 10 weeks. Moe tried to enter, but was rejected by the CPGA because he was not affiliated with a registered club. Coming to his rescue, the sponsor allowed him to enter anyway. And, in an attempt to legalize himself, Moe signed on with a Don Mills driving range as assistant to Bill Mark, the pro there. The CPGA still nixed Moe's attempt at a card because Mark held a U.S. PGA card, not a Canadian one.

He entered the bursary tournament anyway on the sponsor's say-so, hoping public pressure might soften the CPGA's stance if he placed among the top three. After tight play for 36 holes, Moe managed to squeak in as the third-place winner. Fortunate as the win was, the CPGA didn't bend. Moe was not a carded pro and therefore he was ineligible to claim the bursary. He remained in limbo.

Moe Norman did have his supporters in the governing golf establishment, but not enough of them. While they worked on ways to slide Moe into their organization, Moe returned to Florida for another winter. He played more bootleg and earned additional income with impromptu swing demonstrations. Moe relied on spectator generosity as he had done when he was a young amateur. It was a hard few months. The number of "stiffs" had declined as his reputation for skinning the unwary spread at courses in Georgia and Florida.

When spring finally arrived, Moe made his way home again. That April, however, he had something to look forward to. He had signed with CPGA carded pro, Bert Turcotte, at the de Havilland Golf Center in Toronto. Although Turcotte's facility wasn't registered with the CPGA, Turcotte had convinced the powers in charge at the CPGA to allow Moe this chance.

For $50 a week, Moe Norman taught. He gleefully proved to the other club pros (those who worried about his people skills) that they were wrong. Moe enjoyed working with golfers of limited skill. His teaching technique often left much to be desired (he might step in to demonstrate a point of swing mechanics and bang out balls for the student's entire lesson). Regularly, those he booked for the six-dollar lessons complained and demanded refunds from the fast-talking instructor, but Turcotte wasn't concerned. Moe was managing to sell a good chunk of golf equipment and that made up for the lesson credits. Moe augmented his weekly salary with sales commission and often outsold the other five assistants on the staff at de Havilland. He was a dependable worker who took his responsibility as an instructor to heart, even though his simplified teaching methods were difficult for many to follow.

True to his informal agreement with the CPGA, Turcotte tried to help Moe polish his social skills. He taught him how to order meals in upscale restaurants, how to work through a roomful of golfers with small talk, what to say when graciously accepting a prize. What he didn't try to do was change Moe's nature or tone him down. And because of this, Moe Norman opened up to his friend and employer. Turcotte's lifestyle coaching began to pay off. In his first tournament as a pro, the Ontario Open, Moe managed to best his old nemesis Gerry Kesselring, leaving the course politely with $1000.

Sports reporters, however, weren't ready to let the old Moe fade away easily or be replaced by this newer professional version. They watched him, ready to report any antics on the course. Moe was always good for colour and they were hungry to add a little to their tournament coverage. Moe's new serious attitude to the game became grist for copy instead. The reporters noted how he barked at distracting fans around the green or took time to size up even "gimme" putts. It was something the old Moe would never have done. The clown had become serious. Moe won the tournament, and prestigious golf media hailed the victory as the beginning of one of the most "appealing professional careers that the golfing world has ever known."

However, Moe Norman's press status soon faded. The young dapper champ of the 1955 Canadian Junior had also turned pro. George Knudson epitomized the classic pro. His swing was beautiful and fluid. He was a bright conversationalist and a rising golf star. Though Moe could outplay Knudson, and did on two different occasions, he dropped in the press view to second-class status. George looked exactly the way they thought a Canadian professional golfer should. To them, it seemed that Moe was still an unpolished arcane wannabe.

As the British and American Motors Bursary Tournament came around again in August, Moe felt the pressure to succeed just as heavily as he had the first time. His amateur career had been brilliant, but every step of his road to a professional one was hindered. He needed the bursary, and badly, if he was to move forward in his pursuit of status.

The Bursary Tournament audience was treated to excellent golf that year. Moe Norman, his close friend Irv Lightstone, and the cocky young George Knudson all reached the finals. While Norman had beaten Knudson and should have had the confidence of that to push him, Knudson's play that round was daring and his shots accurate. In the face of Knudson's display of skill, Norman seemed to retreat. Nonetheless, he managed to snag third place and capture a spot for a $1500 bursary for the second time.

Some parts of Moe's behaviour changed when he joined the U.S. PGA Tour. For one thing, he reduced his performances for the gallery to only occasional horseplay. But his basic nature was the same. And he still hoarded his money like a miser. Moe's life had always been lived in a hand-to-mouth fashion. Cash was king to Moe, and he loved knowing that he had it on hand. For that reason perhaps, Moe had never opened a bank account. He carried his wealth in his front pants pocket in a bulging wad of rolled $100 bills that spectators often mistook for extra golf balls. The prospect of travelling on the U.S. Tour, however, forced him to make some other basic changes.

In 1958, Moe called upon a director of the Ontario Golf Association, who also happened to be an auto dealer, and ordered a car. A year-old Cadillac was delivered to de Havilland soon after and Moe — unable to even give the vehicle a test drive because he still didn't have a driver's licence — paid for it in cash with 26 of his $100 bills.

Moe had a penchant for big cars, having noticed that his golfing idols drove Cadillacs. To him, it was only fitting that he look the part of their equal by driving one too. The Cadillac offered plenty of room, a powerful and comfortable ride, and a huge trunk. The trunk space was precisely what he needed for the U.S. Tour.

From the day he finally got his driver's licence, Moe's Cadillac did double duty as his home on wheels. Everything he owned found a handy spot either inside the car or in the trunk. Golf supplies; boxes of clothing, books, and magazines; and his cash. Moe used the Cadillac as his bank, the nooks and crannies and the space behind the spare tire becoming his hidden safety-deposit boxes.

# Chapter 8
# Learning the Ropes

Moe Norman's arrival to the U.S. PGA Tour was proclaimed by the golfing press as a breath of freshness in the stultified atmosphere of professional golf. *Golf World* put him on their cover with his collection of oversized tees. The *Toronto Star* wished him luck and the PGA brass told him to mind his Ps and Qs on their turf.

His debut on the U.S. Tour took place at the Rancho Municipal Golf Course for the Los Angeles Open. Moe played his game safe, only surrendering to a vocal gallery once by driving off the big tees. He had a great time chatting with the gallery, even taking a side bet from one of the spectators. Moe managed to hold his nerves in check that day, even though he recognized he was playing with the highest calibre golfers in the world. He finished a long way behind the leader, but that was less important to Moe than the fact he was actually sharing a fairway with him.

The professional golfing fraternity, however, wasn't as happy to have this odd bird splashing around in their bath. After all, Moe still dressed strangely, had a queer way of playing, and seemed never to take the job of pro golf as seriously as everyone else. Around the course he obviously enjoyed himself, but other players had trouble getting to know the newcomer.

Moe continued to be shy and reserved in the locker room and clubhouse. He was nervous and tongue-tied when his idols such as Arnold Palmer and Sam Snead held court. His finances were still lean and didn't allow him to match the wardrobe extravagances he saw among other players. Moe had only a single pair of pants and his shirts were all turtlenecks (in red, blue, and black). Moe saw the other players leaving tips in the clubhouse lounge larger than the cost of most of his meals. He observed their relaxed controlled personas amid the wolf-pack press, and he envied them.

On the course, however, he was the same Moe that Canadian fans had come to love. Any pro who took the time to notice him there or on the driving range was awed by the purity of his swing. And, it wasn't just the accuracy of his swing that prompted Ken Venturi to nickname him Pipeline Moe either. Norman could make the ball move in mid-air like a puppet master. He had a shot for every conceivable circumstance he found himself facing on the course. His long game had every other pro salivating and quietly thanking the universal powers that Moe was such a klutz on the greens. For some reason, Moe still couldn't transform the confidence he exhibited at the tee into his game of inches. Although he had slowed his putting style markedly thanks to Turcotte's advice, he still seemed to rush. It was as if he couldn't bear the pressure of being on stage. There were just too many variables to contend with for his analytical mind. Roll. Hardness. Speed. He let his putter hang loose in his hands, so different for his controlling choke at the tee. He seemed confused on the greens. It all showed, sadly, in his results there. Moe rarely made big dollars that season, ending his take after 10 tournaments in the winter tour at only $1360.

When his first season as a pro ended, Moe returned to his job at de Havilland and again took part in the Bursary Tournament the following August. He snagged third spot for the third time to finance his second season on the winter tour of 1960. However, again, he barely broke even, with only slightly more than $1500 in winnings, the amount of his bursary. After that season, the curtain began to fall. Moe, now too old at 31 years to qualify for another Bursary Tournament, had to rely on his own pocketbook to pay for the tour and he refused to use his own cash. Without a sponsor footing the bill for his expenses, he said he couldn't afford to go.

When other pros on the tour tried to analyze why such a talented golfer couldn't succeed among them, many put it down to his concentration. Moe appeared to lose interest during a round. He'd experiment with different shots just to add some spice to his game. Moe may also have been handicapped by the slow pace of most professional tournaments. When play slowed to a crawl as it so often did, Moe turned into an excited version of himself, pacing as though he was caged. The pros also suspected Moe didn't have the lifeskills required in the rarified atmosphere of elite golf.

Most other pros had been raised to understand that to make money one had to spend it. That was spending for clothes and travel and accommodation. You invested your money in yourself in order to grow your wealth. Moe appeared to be more comfortable saving what he earned, always hoping someone else with more confidence than he had in his skill, would front the risk capital.

A few of the pros, those who did get to understand

the enigma that Moe Norman represented to the world, thought he may also have been lonely. Although he didn't venture out of his safe zone often to make new friends, when he did he was fiercely loyal to them. He wanted to be with them in situations where he felt welcome and loved. On the tour, in circumstances where golfers could smile one minute and then try to psyche opponents out of doing their best the next, Moe may have felt very isolated. Callous competitors didn't hide their disdain for Moe's appearance or his showmanship, which they considered unprofessional. Perhaps Norman came to believe he was unwanted. Perhaps the pros seemed too much like the bullies of the schoolyard and that managed to turn him from his dreams. Moe told his close friends he'd been publicly humiliated by other pros. To others, he simply said it was his putter. Whatever the reason was, in the final analysis it made no difference. Moe decided never to return to the U.S. PGA Tour.

In Ontario, Bert Turcotte had moved to a new range, and when Moe left the tour he joined Turcotte there. Moe seemed to have accepted his own decision and began to proudly describe himself as a teaching pro. He blamed the heavy commitment of time at Pleasure Park, Turcotte's new driving range, as the main reason he didn't play in more tournaments. It was just too hard to play well without regular practice. Applying his focus as a teacher came easily to Moe. Again, he tried to pass on techniques as simply as possible, reflecting his belief that most instructors made the science of the game more complicated that it had to be.

It was three years before Moe made it back to competitive golf. In 1963 he won three major Canadian events including the Saskatchewan Open and his second Ontario Open. At the Canadian Open in Scarboro, the nation was watching. Moe played his first three rounds solidly with even par-71s, and on the final day was clearly being supported by fans even though he was in second place, three strokes behind his U.S. PGA friend David Ford. For the last round, Moe Norman was teamed to play with David Ford and Herman Keiser. Both Norman and Ford were speedy players. They'd finish a practice round in just two hours. Keiser, on the other hand, was a 48-year-old plodder who had won the 1946 Masters and was playing slowly, oblivious to his partner's discomfort.

Keiser's snail-like pace was obviously wearing on Norman's patience. Though Moe was lacing it down the fairways like an aimed cannon, his putting seemed to be getting shakier every hole. Fans were wildly applauding Ford and Keiser but were only offering Moe their encouragement, as though he was second-rate in comparison. The impact of the slow game and Moe's perceptions about the crowd's attitude began to aggregate. By the time the threesome were on the back nine, it was having a visible effect on his game. Perhaps Moe was in his reluctant-winner mode again by then as well. A national championship held extreme dangers for him psychologically, in that he knew winners quickly vaulted to star status and the limelight. Limelight was something Moe tried to avoid. He might have been considering the negative side of that notoriety as he played. Through the back nine, Moe putted with unusual haste. The results were sad, and disappointing for the gallery. Nevertheless, Moe was still only trailing Ford by a few strokes.

On the 15th tee, the pressure valve in Moe finally blew. Ford and Keiser had poor drives. When Moe approached the tee, a probably well-meaning fan shouted for the turtle-necked striker to show the other pros how a drive should be hit. Moe reacted immediately. He dropped his driver where he stood and loudly berated the gallery for their poor show of sportsmanship and golfing etiquette. Then Moe hit and, as usual, stitched one down the centre of the fairway. The moment at the tee box had riled him immensely and for some reason he couldn't let it go. As he played, his anger continued to boil. His game, as a result, abruptly began to deflate and he finished the round with a 75, an embarrassing eight shots behind the leader that netted him only $625 for the effort.

Moe, as usual, went back south. Two people he met there, Orm and Verna Membery, took a chance on him in 1965. The Memberys owned a 6400-yard public course called Golf Haven in Gilford, a pleasant community north of Toronto, and they hired him as their pro. As the club pro, Moe represented Golf Haven in tournaments and he had time to practice his game without the heavy teaching schedule he'd had at Pleasure Park. It was a year for tuning his game again. Moe was genuinely happy, even though he won only the Manitoba Open that year. He felt safe and comfortable with the Memberys, whom he came to look upon as family. He called Verna "Mom" and opened himself to her, confiding secret hopes for his life that he'd kept locked from the rest of the world.

Verna helped Moe in countless ways, just as Turcotte had years before. Turcotte, however, had done much of his advising out of kindness while Verna did it out of love. She slowly eased Moe into accepting social situations more readily, and she guided him with his wardrobe. Moe responded like a flower after a rain. He began winning again and feeling confident in himself and his value as a person. When Moe reportedly was

carrying all his winnings in his pocket — $20,000 worth
— it was Verna who finally convinced him to rent a safe-
ty deposit box in a bank. She also helped him get settled
in a permanent room of his own in Aurora, Ontario.

Moe had a habit of replacing his Cadillac with a
newer model each year. In the summer of 1966 he set
out in his latest car to play in tournaments across
Canada and the United States. It was a phenomenal year
for him, a year that harkened back to his more vibrant
and carefree times as a fun-loving amateur. He won five
major events including the Quebec, Manitoba, and
Alberta Opens. That summer he had his biggest ever
payday thus far in his career when he won the Willow
Park Classic Pro-Am and its prize purse of $5000. In
Calgary, he reminded the CPGA that he was a golfer to
be reckoned with as a professional. Also held at Willow
Park, the CPGA championship was a sweet victory. All
told, Moe headed back to Golf Haven after that summer
with winnings of over $13,000.

Moe claimed he had saved $40,000, which was con-
siderably more than he'd need to return to the U.S. PGA
Tour, but he was still unwilling to invest it in himself. If
he had a sponsor to "share the risk," he said, he would
try again but only then. Having won the CPGA champi
onship, Moe was immediately qualified to play in the
Canadian Open but he declined, opting to play in a

smaller event in Rochester, New York instead.

One more time he'd thumbed his nose at the golfing establishment, even if unintentionally. One more time the golfing powers-that-be fumed. Some pros in the organization demanded Moe's suspension for the insult to the CPGA, but the Professional Golfers' Association was more politically astute. Moe was verbally reprimanded for embarrassing his association, but little else was done to punish him.

Early that September, he was named to be part of the Canadian group that travelled to England to compete in the Carling World Championship. Moe may have hoped the tournament would attract a sponsor. Perhaps he thought it might also patch up any bad feelings in the CPGA. What he didn't factor was the difference in attitude in England concerning playing style. The gallery welcomed his play with as much enthusiasm as they would the flu. Moe, still hypersensitive to strangers' criticisms, showed his hurt feelings when he overheard rude and cruel assessments of his style and lacklustre performance.

Even so, he made the cut. He finished the final round 13 shots behind the leader, but captured the status of top Canadian. Back home, the press trumpeted his victory again and forecast that the boy from Kitchener had proven himself worthy of the U.S. PGA one more time. "Moe is back," they hinted. "The best is yet to come." It even appeared as though golf's blue-bloods were willing to forgive and forget as well. But the cards just weren't falling right.

The CPGA Championship had also qualified Moe to represent Canada as part of a two-man team at the Canada Cup (now World Cup) in Tokyo. It was slated for November, but Moe didn't receive his invitation until mid-September, *after* returning from England and months following his CPGA win in Calgary. In the interim, he had made arrangements to play in the Pan-American Tour.

When the CPGA invite arrived, the conflict threw Moe into a confused state of uncertainty. He'd committed himself to Seagram's Ltd. for the Pan-American Tour. Perhaps he hoped they might become his long-hoped-for sponsor and didn't want to offend them by cancelling in order to play in the Canada Cup. Not knowing what he should do, Moe's choice was to cancel both tours.

The crevice between Moe and the CPGA, as a result, was now so wide that it looked like it might never be bridged again. Not long after his decision not to play in Tokyo was announced, the CPGA held an award dinner to honour the nation's top golfers. Moe had won the A.T. Hunt Trophy for low-scoring average (the third such win of his career) but he didn't attend to receive it. That must have done it for many in the CPGA. Moe's future with the press, as well as with the CPGA, looked bleak. Moe didn't seem to mind. He was doing well on most other fronts during the 1960s. He was still winning tournaments, just not as many. In 1967, with his arm ringed in watches, Moe won the Manitoba Open for the third time in a row, collecting $16,000 in prize money.

In 1968, he won $11,000, which he reportedly carried with him. Moe was managing to live well, though simply. He subsisted during the day on Coke and junk food and he ate one large wholesome meal a day. On the road he found low-cost motels or, when rooms weren't available, stretched his 200-pound frame on the back seat of his car.

During the 1960s, Moe began to take his game more seriously than ever. His notoriety resulted in some problems with distraction during play, and he often reacted rudely. As an amateur, he had found pleasure in chatting with fans as he played. Now all he wanted was silence. Fans were not encouraged to walk with him. The fans could be served up a verbal reprimand if the gallery didn't hold its breath when it was his turn to putt. His putting style had never changed, but Moe had. He still played fast and putted loose, but he wanted and expected the elusive element of respect he saw other well-known players receiving from their fans.

The CPGA finally called Moe Norman on his surly attitude. Following the 1968 Canadian Tour championship, the CPGA held a meeting about him. Several of the pros attending the hearing wanted Moe's head on a platter. They called for his suspension, claiming his conduct was giving the tour and professional golf a bad name. Moe was fined for "verbal improprieties" and required to give back a part of his winnings from the tournament. It amounted to 10 percent, and was the largest fine the CPGA had ever given a player.

Moe suffered in other ways, too. Fewer clubs were willing to invite him to play in their events, while a few professionals offered the worst insult of all: they refused to be seen with him. Fortunately for the golf world, it wasn't everyone.

In 1969, Sam Snead and Ed (Porky) Oliver agreed to play with him in an exhibition in Toronto. The round was one of those casual games that added another notch to the Moe Norman legend. During the exhibition play, the threesome had reached a hole that featured a creek cutting the fairway about 240 yards from the tee. Snead and Oliver looked at the hazard and decided the best play was to lay up. Moe reached for his driver. Snead, always a gentleman, graciously reminded Moe about the creek and suggested it wouldn't be possible to clear it with a driver. "Not trying to," Norman said. "I'm playing for the bridge." Moe set up, eyed his target and fired. His ball floated through the air with its character-istic "Moe spin," then softly dropped short of the creek and gently rolled forward over the bridge to the other side. Snead, the man who'd given some kind advice on swing correction at Norman's Masters debut, didn't say a word for the rest of the round.

The greats viewed Norman's skill as magical. Moe didn't set out to be irascible on the course, but still, he did things that fed the impression that he was the *bad boy* of the Canadian Tour. For example, he often turned from strangers when they spoke to him, clearly sig-nalling he didn't care to speak. And he refused to sign autographs unless it was a child making the request (sometimes he'd also give them a golf ball as a memen-to). To young pros on the tour, Moe was always willing to offer advice that might improve their game. Sometimes, if he thought a golfer was serious about his goals, he would pass over a gift of cash to help along the way. Stories about Moe's generosity to other players on the tour have been embellished over time, but the essence of them is true. In addition, he would lend his always-ready cash to others freely, often never seeing the loans repaid.

In 1971, when he was 42 years old, Moe decided he

was going to cut his summer schedule of golf in Canada
way back. Instead of returning in April as he had always
done, he stayed in Florida until the middle of July. He
said he planned on playing only tournaments closer to
home, complaining that there was no longer any incen-
tive for travelling across Canada to play. He'd won all the
tournaments anyway.

At that time, Imperial Tobacco was deploying its
promotional power in a number of sporting and entertainment venues. Golf was one. Imperial Tobacco had
decided to sponsor the Canadian Tour, renaming it the
Peter Jackson Tour, and contributing $78,000 in prize
money to be spread over seven events. They used their
Player's brand to sponsor motor racing and du Maurier
became the saviour of the struggling arts community.

Imperial Tobacco hired the nation's leading sports
public relations firm, The Houston Group, to promote
their program. The public relations staff of The Houston
Group organized the advance media blitz, operated the
media room, and even filed radio and newspaper
reports on each event for media who couldn't afford to
send their own reporters. The Houston Group team
worked hard, and successfully lured Moe Norman.

He played the first tournament that year, the
Ontario Open, which offered a $16,000 purse. And he
bombed. Moe's game had taken a weird left turn and

he knew it. He recanted on his decision not to travel, perhaps pushed by his desire to regain his swing, perhaps because some stalwart supporters during his bid for professional status were among the organizers.

He followed the Ontario debacle with a win at the Alberta Open and then lost the Manitoba Open in a playoff with Florida's John Elliott. The reason for the loss was a bizarre rule infraction, and Moe should have known better. The match was a stroke-play event. On the second extra-hole, Moe ran his ball to within a few inches of the cup and Elliott, jokingly, told his redheaded opponent to pick it up. Perhaps Moe forgot the rules. When he scooped up his ball he was immediately disqualified. The gallery and the sponsor loudly argued that the disqualification was unfair. After some heated discussions with the tournament officials, Moe was allowed to put his ball back and tap it in. Sponsorship money — more than the rule book — held sway in the game that day. Moe was recognized as a star attraction. He drew huge crowds and Imperial Tobacco wasn't blind to that fact. Norman was the top money leader that year, earning $7000, and gaining back certainty about his game.

This wasn't apparent at the Quebec Open...but it sure was a week later at the 1971 Canadian Open. In Quebec, he reached the final hole with a one-stroke lead but four-putted to finish in second. His playing partner, Gary Slatter, said Moe had been upset by the gallery. They hadn't responded in applause as he approached the green. Moe felt they should have, as he was the only player to have reached it in two that day.

In the practice round for the Canadian Open, while Moe approached the tee of a 233-yard par-3, a reporter made a wisecrack about the putting travesty. Moe reacted with silence, the redness in his face spreading to the back of his neck. He teed up, found his target, and gave the ball a crack. He watched it as it flew towards the green and then turned to the reporter. "Not putting today," he said cryptically. The reporter watched as the ball landed at the front of the green and rolled into the cup.

When the 1971 season ended, Moe withdrew from playing tournaments. Perhaps he was simply tired of the grind. Perhaps he was content with the mechanical perfection of his swing. Perhaps he was looking deeper for the roots of excellence, because in 1973, Moe encountered a philosophy — one that described what he had been doing all his life. Irv Schloss, the man behind the creation of the PGA Merchandise Show held every year for club pros across the continent, was one of the first men to embrace technology to analyze and correct swing defaults. He filmed swings. He was also a proponent of theories that tied the mental visualization of success to the act of golfing.

Moe was excited by Schloss's theories. The psychology of success mirrored his subconsciously chosen method of teaching his body the perfect swing. He began to study the various avenues of the theory, latching comfortably onto motivational teachings. He would often drive his Cadillac into the Florida night, with audio tapes playing, constantly in search of the parallels between what was being taught and the mental side of golf. To Moe, the process was an epiphany. He began to realize that life could be understood and managed with a "knowing" outlook. He began compiling inspirational sayings and reading about the mental dynamics of sport performance. On the course, and at tournaments he played only occasionally, he tried to pass on what he was learning.

Many of those he cornered in his zeal to share were taken aback. They didn't feel Moe understood what he was proclaiming. But to him their reaction now made no difference. Moe was becoming comfortable in his body and, for the first time, had begun to understand his feelings. All his life he'd considered himself less intelligent than those around him. Now he realized it was because his mind worked in a different way. The realization was like opening a window in a stuffy room.

Moe's shyness became less obvious and he was able to more readily control his emotions. He was more prepared to speak in public, and the following year willingly gave his first clinic for a fee at the Bayview Club in Toronto. In the past, Moe might have offered a demonstration of his swing at the driving range to an always-ready crowd, but he would have done little more than hit balls. Now he spoke about the mental aspect of the game as well as his technique. He became focused on the *essence* of technique rather than the *demonstration* of it.

In 1974, Moe finished second on the Canadian Tour money list, winning $11,500. In the years that followed, he was a regular fixture on the tour but never a winner again...until the 1976 Alberta Open. He played his last Canadian Tour tournament the next year by winning the Atlantic Open, just as Imperial Tobacco decided to drop its sponsorship of the Peter Jackson Tour.

# Chapter 9
# A Helping Hand

The next decade was lean for Moe Norman. Tournament winnings to be had were few and far between. Moe gained weight and slipped into debt. Three decades of living hand-to-mouth had become the norm for him, but now creeping up to 50, it was taking a toll on his health. His friends worried and tried to encourage him, but Moe had become a shadow of his younger self.

In 1985 he won the CPGA Seniors Championship for the sixth time and pocketed a $3500 cheque, but money earned at other tournaments was meagre. Things could have been better. Sam Snead was leading a group of older PGA pros in a drive to create a Senior

PGA Tour. Moe was repeatedly invited to participate but always refused, saying he needed a sponsor. This was puzzling to his friends. Some of them were certain several potential sponsors had stepped forward to back him on the Senior Tour, but nothing had ever come of the apparent overtures.

It got worse for Moe. The following year his finances crashed. For the first time in seven years, Moe lost the CPGA Seniors Championship, and without that injection of cash he was facing $20,000 in debts and financial ruin. The bank was even threatening to repossess his car because he was behind in his monthly payments.

About that time, Moe told the *Kitchener–Waterloo Record* that it was like moving backwards to the days when he was a junior without money. "I don't have two nickels to rub together," he told the newspaper. "It's been a nice recess for 30 years, but now it's over and it doesn't look like it's going to get any better." He told another newspaper, "It's tough to do things when you're broke. Hitchhiking to tournaments, sleeping on park benches, sleeping in bunkers. I slept in bunkers all over Canada."

With his trip to Florida in serious jeopardy for the first time in his life, Moe's friends decided to act. A fundraising golf tournament and dinner organized by

Gus and Audrey Maue in September raised $26,000 for Moe in one night. It was an amazing outpouring of generosity by the many people Moe had helped and touched during his lifetime. Moe was able to pay all his debts and it lifted him emotionally. He allowed his friends to help him open a bank account. And he began giving clinics again. As clubs heard he was available, offers started to increase and so did his financial footing.

After his Florida sojourn in 1987, Moe returned to Canada in high form. He was hitting the ball well again, some said as well as he ever had, and he proved it by winning the CPGA's Senior Tournament handily. But the reprieve of money from the fundraiser and the $9500 he earned at the tournament only went so far. For an old golfer with no retirement plan, the future was still very dark. But his legend lived on through television, through the pages of the golfing media, and through laudatory comments by golfing greats such as Lee Trevino. In 1988, Trevino told *The Fifth Estate* that Moe was a special man. "I do not know any player who could strike a golf ball like he can, as far as hitting it solid, knowing where it's going, knowing the mechanics of the game, and knowing what he wanted to do with the golf ball." Trevino repeated his adulation a year later, in May 1989, when he told *Golf Magazine* that Moe was "a genius when it comes to playing the game of golf."

Moe, photographed in 1986

Moe, on the advice of his friend and unofficial manager Gus Maue, focused his efforts on his clinics. His popularity there was growing. By 1992 his cost of putting on the clinics in different cities was matched by his income and, starting in 1993, he began to see a profit. That year he was able to do 70 clinics, collecting about $900 for each. Things began to look up. Moe was building his savings. An importer in Edmonton signed Moe to a line of golf gear. The press rediscovered him — again — and Moe finally found a sponsor.

Jack Kuykendall had independently developed a swing system that matched the one Moe had built for himself and he called it Natural Golf. Natural Golf hired Moe on a three-year exclusive contract to demonstrate his single-axis swing with different training products.

Then, in 1995, his luck and his world really turned around. That February the CEO and President of Titleist and FootJoy Worldwide, Wally Uihlein, read in the *Wall Street Journal* about Kuykendall's discovery of a new golf swing, and that Moe Norman was under contract to his company. Uihlein approached Kuykendall to see if Natural Golf would allow Titleist to make a video of Moe's swing as a record for posterity. They also wanted to recognize Moe Norman's contribution to the sport with a $5000 a month pension. "I've seen too many of the legends of golf spend their last few days on poverty row and in destitution and I don't think it's right," he said.

When Uihlein and Kuykendall approached him with the offer, Moe was naturally suspicious. "I've played your balls all my life, I wear your shoe," he said.

"What do I have to do for that?" Uihlein told him Titleist just wanted to say thank you "for what you have already done." Moe asked the same question again and got the same answer before he would believe his good fortune. Moe had no obligation to Titleist, and the company had no plans of exploiting Moe for commercial purposes. It was simply a gesture of generosity for a player that Uihlein felt exhibited the purest swing of any golfer on earth.

Moe Norman finally made the grade with the RCGA on February 20, 1995, when it was announced he had been elected to the Canadian Golf Hall of Fame. His election was the result of a nomination received from Nick Weslock two years earlier. Moe said he felt his life was vindicated by the honour because he believed that public pressure finally made the RCGA give in and recognize him as the man with the purist swing.

Almost a year later to the month, Moe Norman and Gary Cowan were offered exemptions into the 78-player field for the du Maurier Champions, the RCGA's national senior professional championship. Gary accepted the exemption to play in the $1.1-million U.S. Senior PGA Tour event. Moe did not.

Moe continued to spend his winters in east central Florida, staging free golf clinics with his friend and fellow instructor, Craig Shankland, proprietor of Ocean

Palm Golf Course in Flagler Beach and Hidden Lakes Golf Course in New Smyrna Beach. Moe would step onto the range and begin to hit his volley of shots, mixing them with his maxims for golf and his phrases of self-adulation. "I'm the best ball striker by far. No one else is close," he would say. "No wasted motion. That's why I'm the best ball striker there is. I see only one thing after each shot. Happiness." He'd hit the balls and smile.

"M--0–S. More of the same," he'd say. "More of the same."

# Epilogue

During his summer in Canada in 1997, Moe Norman suffered a coronary while driving. He was taken from Kitchener to the London Health Sciences Centre for coronary bypass surgery.

When noting Moe's considerable distress brought on by his strange surroundings and his extreme fear of surgery, the medical staff tried to determine his mental state by asking him if he knew where he was. "The third hole," he answered confidently.

Moe's answer caused the staff concern until one medic remembered something from way back. The part of the hospital they were in had been built where the third hole of the London Hunt Club had once been located. Moe had played the course. Forty years before. It proved one more time that Moe had an amazing memory — and that his whole life was tied unalterably to golf.

In October 2003, he suffered another attack, which was reported as congestive heart failure. At the time of this writing, Moe Norman is still in recovery. His skill and his unique brand of independence will always be remembered by anyone who strides onto a tee and begins an internal dialogue.

*"Just a walk in the park, walk in the park."*

# Moe Norman's Career Achievements

Moe set 33 course records, and shot 17 hole-in-ones (eight of them on the fly). He set amazing records with three 59 scores during tournament play and had four double eagles. He was inducted into the Canadian Hall of Fame in 1995.

1954  America's Cup Canadian Team Member

1955  Canadian Amateur Champion

1956  Canadian Amateur Champion

1957  Runner-Up Low Canadian Open

1958  Canadian Open

1958  Ontario Open Champion

1963  Saskatchewan Open Champion

1963  Ontario Open Champion

1964  CPGA Miller Trophy Champion

1965  Manitoba Open Champion

1965  Runner-up Canadian Professional Golfers' Championship

1966  Canadian Professional Golfers Champion

1966  Alberta Open

1966  Quebec Open Champion
1966  Manitoba Open Champion
1967  Manitoba Open Champion
1968  Saskatchewan Open Champion
1971  Alberta Open Champion
1971  World Cup National Team
1974  Canadian Professional Golfers' Champion
1976  Alberta Open Champion
1980  Canadian Professional Golfers' Association
1981  Canadian Senior Championship
1982  Canadian Senior Championship
1983  Canadian Senior Championship
1984  Canadian Senior Championship
1985  Canadian Senior Championship
1987  Canadian Senior Championship

# Bibliography

Canadian Broadcasting Corporation. "Moe Norman: The King of Swing." CBC *Life and Times*, Toronto: CBC. Original air date March 19, 2002.

Fidlin, Ken. "One Moe Time: Still the Man: Norman continues to wow 'em like no one else." Toronto: Ontario in the *Toronto Sun*. 2002.

O'Connor, Tim. "The Feeling of Greatness: The Moe Norman Story." Mississauga, Ontario: Eyelevel Videos Inc., 1995.

O'Connor, Tim. "Heroes of Golf: Moe Norman Straight Down the Pipe." in *LINKS Magazine*, Hilton Head Island, South Carolina. August 1997.

Warters, John. "Legendary Moe Norman: Still Giving Clinics" in *Florida Golf News*, Daytona Beach, Florida. January 1999.

Zasky, Jason. "Moe Norman: The greatest golfer the world has never known" in *Failure Magazine*, Chestnut Ridge, New York, July 2000.

# Acknowledgments

I'd like to acknowledge the poignant biography on Moe Norman produced by CBC Television, and I highly recommend Tim O'Connor's book *The Feeling of Greatness: The Moe Norman Story.* The latter is a sensitively written account that offers a detailed perspective of the impact Moe Norman's unique persona had on the sport.

# About the Author

Stan Sauerwein lives and writes in Westbank, British Columbia. A freelance writer for two decades, his articles have appeared in a variety of Canadian and U.S. magazines and newspapers. Specializing in business subjects, he has written for both corporations and governments. He is the author of four other books – *Rattenbury: The Life and Tragic End of B.C.'s Greatest Architect*; *Ma Murray: The Story of Canada's Crusty Queen of Publishing*; *Klondike Joe Boyle: Heroic Adventures From Gold Fields to Battlefields*; and *Fintry: Lives, Loves and Dreams*.

# Photo Credits

All photographs are reproduced courtesy of the Canadian Golf Hall of Fame Archives.

AMAZING STORIES™

# MA MURRAY

The Story of Canada's
Crusty Queen of Publishing

HISTORY/BIOGRAPHY
by Stan Sauerwein

ISBN 1-55153-979-9

# BY THE SAME AUTHOR

AMAZING STORIES™

## KLONDIKE JOE BOYLE

Heroic Adventures From
Gold Fields to Battlefields

HISTORY/BIOGRAPHY
by Stan Sauerwein

ISBN 1-55153-969-1

# OTHER AMAZING STORIES

These titles are available wherever you buy books. If you have trouble finding the book you want, call the Altitude order desk at 1-800-957-6888, e-mail your request to: orderdesk@altitudepublishing.com or visit our Web site at www.amazingstories.ca

New AMAZING STORIES titles are published every month. If you would like more information, e-mail your name and mailing address to: amazingstories@altitudepublishing.com.